WOULDN'T BE DEAD FOR QUIDS

(AN INDULGENCE IN RHYME)

BOB MENZIES

Published in Australia by Sid Harta Publishers Pty Ltd,
ABN: 34 632 585 203
17 Coleman Parade, GLEN WAVERLEY VIC 3150 Australia
Telephone: +61 3 9560 9920, Facsimile: +61 3 9545 1742
E-mail: author@sidharta.com.au

First published in Australia 2020
This edition published 2020

Cover design, typesetting: WorkingType (www.workingtype.com.au)

Menzies, R.F.
Wouldn't Be Dead for Quids
ISBN: 978-1-925707-30-4
pp290

About the Author

Bob Menzies was born in Seymour, Victoria. His father was in the army which resulted in Bob being educated in various schools and colleges around Australia. After he finished school, he joined the Royal Australian Navy where he spent 14 years travelling around the world. After this, he spent 14 years with the South Australian Correctional Services Department reaching the position of Manager. When Bob retired from this part of his life, he started writing and continues to do so to this day. Bob lives with his wife, Heather, in the mountains just out of Melbourne.

Acknowledgments

Thank you to David & Patsy Bean for their support and friendship and above all encouraging me to write.

Special thanks must also go to my Publisher Kerry Collison, my Editor Barbara Ivusic and to the hard work and tolerance of Luke Harris the Typesetter.

Finally I'd like to thank Jessica Walley for her 'IT' help & support.

Index

An indulgence 1
Childhood 2
Grandpa and Nan's 3
Cars 5
Passing Cars 6
Vermin 8
Rabbits 9
Policing 11
Road Kill 12
Armed Services 14
Anal-Retentive 15
How do you feel? 17
Belle of the Ball 18
The Innocent 20
Victim Status 21
Enjoy it 23
Some 24
Zoos 26
Gaze In Wonder 27
The Parent Trap 29
Upstairs/Downstairs 30
The Price You Pay 32
Redemption 33
A Night Out 35
Social Confusion 36

True Blue 38
A Country Boy 39
Learning 41
Bulletproof 42
Never Forget 44
Chain Reaction 45
Love Story 47
Words On the Wind 48
Cruising The Murray 50
River Ramble 51
Just A Thought 55
Leading the Way 56
Boundary Rider 57
Dreaming 59
Pillows 60
From the Heart 62
Questions 63
Friends 64
Assertion 65
Life 67
Doors 68
Writer's Block 70
Lost The Gift 71
Found It 73
Writing Again 74
Warning Signs 76
The Fight 78
Eulogy 81
Close the Windows 82
Right Crosses & Upper Cuts 84
Demons 85
Suckerpunch 87
Perdition 89
Just A Thought 92
Safe Haven 93
Daw Park 94
Roller-Coaster 96
Daylight 97

Anger 99
Do Not Disturb 100
Family 102
Left Of Centre 103
Self Doubt 105
Tug Of War 106
Troughs 108
Quick Fix 109
Just A Thought 112
Meeting Place 114
The Cave 115
Diggers 117
Farm Boy 118
Recognition 120
Long, Black Clouds 121
Understanding 123
Steps 124
Realisation 126
Fear 127
Hiding 129
Fire In The Belly 131
Nightmares 133
The Penny 134
They're Good! 139
The Trip 140
Twilight Zone 142
Limbo 143
Dad 145
Victims 146
Just A Thought 153
Party Time 154
Cassie and Frank's 156
Just A Thought 159
Equality 160
The Dole 161
Author! Author! 163
Mathew Flinders' Cat 164
Harping 166

The Thousand Yard Stare 167
Decisions 169
The Committee 170
Just A Thought 174
Angel 175
The Guardian 176
Letting Go 178
Moving On 179
Cruising Again 181
Frank, Bazz & Pies 182
Busy 187
Rest 188
Solid 190
Unconditional 191
Camping 193
Fingers Of Night 194
Characters 196
The Stampede 197
Just Sitting 202
Embers 203
Stumbling Along 205
Mistakes 206
Cobwebs 208
Ghost Town 209
Perfect 211
The Broken Bucket 212
Just A Thought 215
The River Murray 216
The Hundred Year Drought 217
Get Over It 219
Cyclonic 220
Organised 222
Plans 223
Hit The Road 225
No Fixed Abode 226
Travelin' Around 228
Stairway To Heaven 229
Upside Down 231

The Down Under Dunny 232
Welcome 234
Doorway To The Past 235
Gympie Muster 237
The Hole In The Ground 238
It's Out There Somewhere 240
Gold 241
History 243
Two Lines 244
Reliability 246
The Commer 247
Movin' 'Round 249
The Drifter 250
Bazz & Bob 252
On The Road Again 253
Respect 255
Eternal Soldier 256
Observe 258
Watch 259
Crumbling 261
Rod 262
Just A Thought 265
Crashing 266
Roma 267
Scared 269
Health 270
Just A Thought 273
Great Place 274
Harrow 275
Finale 277
Wouldn't Be Dead For Quids 279
Relapsus Resurgem 281

An indulgence

I am not famous. I have not reached any pinnacles nor climbed any mountains. I have not set any records and I can't build empires.

I am not particularly well educated and I am not a professor of the English language, as you will find out when you read through this book.

What I am is a plain man who has discovered that he has the ability to put down in words what he is actually feeling. I write in 'rhyme' which, at times, may test your patience but the beauty of reading is that you can put the book down and return to it later on.

My indulgence is that a 'nobody' has dared to throw his thoughts onto the open market for all to read. The writings may not be grammatically correct or phrased correctly, but that wasn't my intent. I merely wanted to write things down as I experienced them.

As I have said, I am not famous but the feelings and emotions expressed within these pages are mine and come from a lifetime of observations and experiences that I now invite you all to share ...

— Bob Menzies

Childhood

The fondest memory from everyone's childhood would surely be of their grandparents.

I'm sure that we can all remember when we visited Nana and Pop's place. It was a place where we received hugs and cuddles whilst enjoying those special little treats our parents wouldn't let us have, like sweets, chocolates, ice cream and unconditional love.

But as you get older and busier, you lose the time to visit them as much as you'd like to.

When you do occasionally visit, it is only fleetingly as you can't afford to stay too long because of the kids, your work, living requirements, etc.

You realise how much older they are getting and how much you have forgotten about what they once gave you.

Grandpa and Nan's

Eight forty-five and we'll be arriving — not before then
Knock on the door; we'll be dancing 'til four in the morning
Stoke wood on the old fireplace for keeping us warm like it should
There's happiness about the place, we all feel life is good

Nine forty-two and there's so much to do, it's a party
Looking at you I can see how it all first started
The homestead is so full of love and we're all so happy again
Look at the stars up above — it's great here at Grandpa and Nan's

We're glad that we came as the house looks the same as always
Shots of Grandpa and Nan. In the shots, they ran down the hallway.
They love in every way yet, they're alone every day, must be painful.
The future's not clear 'cos we're not here every year — how hurtful

Our love carries on, although time marches on for our grand-folk
They're steadfast and true with a strength through and through –
like old oak
They've led the way with advice every day from the garden
Now it's their time of need and we rush with all speed,
with the children

We owe it all to those two down the hall for their wisdom
We see them clear although just once a year at reunions
We'd like to visit more as we walk out the door of Grandpa's
They'd like it too, but what else can you do when home's too far

Well time's moving on and the family have gone to the motel
Now that they've gone, we'll be moving on so farewell
But we'll be back again next year to visit Grandpa and Nan
Now all we've got to fear is not doing all that we can

Our time will come when the children will run down the hallway
We'll see them clear although just once a year as always
A year turns to two but what else can you do, but live for them
They'll make our day when next they stay, but not before then.

Cars

Whilst on the subject of Nanna and Pop's place, I can easily remember the quiet ambience of their farm and the simple life they led. It was nothing to get up early to milk the cows or to come home soaking after attempting to drench the sheep. It was a quiet peaceful place that was trapped in a time-warp of days gone by.

I especially remember Pop sitting by the fire, lighting his pipe and telling me of the 'old days' before the advent of motor cars and the need for fuel. He told me that when he first saw a car, he thought that life as he knew it would never be the same. How right he was.

Passing Cars

I saw a car passing by
And a tear welled up in my eye
For, although it was travelling fast
It brought back thoughts of the past

Of times when a horse and a dray
Was all you needed to get through the day
Of times when you'd stop for a chat or
said 'hello' with a tip of your hat

When you knew everyone in town
Where no one would let you down
Of picnics by the creek
Where the whole community would meet

You'd happily run to the store
And didn't mind doing your chores
You loved your mum and your dad
For caring when things got bad

You didn't have a care in the world
You got along — each boy and girl
And after fights in the old school yard
You'd make up — wasn't that hard

Oh, to think of the long lost past
But those memories are fading fast
For the future is a silly season
Where we fight — no rhyme — no reason

Yes, the years have taken their toll
On mankind and all that we hold
The lights of the past are now dim
With a dark future closing in

Another car has just passed me by
Another tear has welled in my eye

Vermin

Growing up in the country certainly makes you appreciate what you have and how to handle adversity.

Drought has always been a part of my life as it has for many others around our drying country.

I can remember a very severe drought that occurred during my teenage years that lasted for only three years, but took its toll on our family in terms of food we could eat.

We couldn't grow crops or vegetables and we couldn't rely on meat from our animals as there was none, so we resorted to eating vermin which, at first, was alright but after three years of eating nothing but rabbit ...

Rabbits

Some said it was the worst of all time
When cattle and sheep would lose their meat
And fish were hard to find
We had little to eat in this fearsome heat

In the years to sixty-nine
So we resorted to eating rabbits
They didn't really seem to mind

We'd set our traps in the morning
And clear them late at night
Tho' some times without warning
We'd shoot the vermin on sight

We'd skin and clean whilst able
Working with all our might
To ensure food was on the table

Morning, noon and night
Now, what mum could do with those rabbits
Was a sight for all to see

From roasting as a habit
To rabbit fricassee
From hare and rabbit patties

To rabbit stew for tea
By the time those years were over
I'd had enough, you see

So don't ever try to feed me rabbit or a hare
For the reply that I might give you
Might be more than you could bear

I think it's high time we gathered
Let's do it without a care
Let's round up those English rodents
And send them back over there.

Policing

As a lad growing up in a country town you certainly got to know your local policeman and he certainly got to know you and your family.

In fact, it was not unusual to see him in your back yard, in civvies, at a barbeque with your parents and sharing a drink with other members of the community. It was a comforting feeling for both the populace and the local 'copper'.

Somewhere along the line we lost this feeling when they stopped being policemen and started becoming revenue raisers.

Road Kill

In the cities, in the towns and in the country too
We were sure all along with the things that we done
And felt a lot safer too

We could travel through life without much strife
— not a mark on the blotter
This left us in good like we knew that it would
When dealing with the local copper

You'd see him each day in his own casual way taking care
of our neighbourhood
He'd stay on his feet whilst walking the beat
Ensuring safety when he could

In the pub with a wink — if you'd had too much drink —
he'd quietly ask you please
To make your way home — stagger off all alone
But first I'll hang onto your keys

He'd look with a frown at a stranger in town
and would know just what to do
To make sure all was right all through the night
Till the stranger would pass through

Not too much went wrong while his presence was on, of that I can
safely say for we lived in a time — I'm not spinning a line
Where we were safer from day to day

Then someone said, "Hell, this is working too well but it doesn't pay
the dues to pay for the way to build every day
There's much more that we can do"

"With things to be done we raise much more funds, how's this for an
appetiser let's raise revenue for the things that we do
Let's invent a breathalyser"

With a heavy load the police share the road saving lives if they can
by hiding with stealth while raising some wealth
For the local government man

They've forgotten our homes and our protective domes without our
local 'bill' He's 'out there' and we're left bare
It's home safety they have killed

Armed Services

The latter years of my youth were spent learning how to be a 'fighting man' in our armed services.

The first thing they drilled into us was the importance of keeping everything neat and tidy. Hell, they were obsessive about it. Just get caught with one article of clothing ironed incorrectly or a speck of dust on the floor and you found yourself doubling around a parade ground with a full backpack and an SLR rifle, which had to be carried above your head, for hours.

I remember thinking that if they ever sent me to war, I at least would be fit enough to outrun the enemy.

You'd think that after serving fourteen years under this regime I would turn into a slob when I 'got out'. I couldn't and still can't get out of the habit. They drilled it into me.

Anal-Retentive

Put them in a row
All your socks
Make sure they're stowed
Just like your jocks

Make sure the shirts
You wear day to day
Are all facing
The same old way

A place for everything
And all in its place
Must be tidy
Must keep up the pace

The plates and saucers
All nice and neat
Just like they 'oughta'
In case you meet

Another repressive
And invite them home
And all's out of order
Like unsightly foam

Make sure you wear
An impressive suit
Because all will care
If you look 'u-beaut'

Try to be normal
And be inventive
Or is it easier
Being anal-retentive?

How do you feel?

As a young bloke from the farm I was pretty naive about life when I first entered the services. Let's face it, I knew nothing.

So it came as a bit of a shock to hear men, who had been in the services a fair while, bragging about their conquests on the sexual front, even the married ones. It seemed, at the time, that women were fair game for these guys.

They would compare notes on each other's conquests and pass on addresses and phone numbers of those they thought were 'certainties'.

It seemed to me that I might as well have been at a cattle market and I used to wonder how these women felt after a night out with one of these so-called studs.

Belle of the Ball

He said he loved you
The feeling's grand
Or is this only a one night stand?

He's placed you above him
For a night or more
Do you feel like a princess or a one night whore?

How do you feel?
The morning after
The night before when things seemed brighter

You met him once
And you loved him twice
Is the morning after really worth the price?

Do you wake up in the morning
With a fog around your head?
There's a new day dawning and a stranger in bed

Where there's no love at all
You're not belle of the ball
It felt so good
With this brand new man
But is he really doing the best that he can

To make you feel like
The belle of the ball
It's so hard to dance when you feel two feet small

He said he loved you
The feeling's grand
But is this only a one night stand?

He's placed you above him For a night or more
Do you feel like a princess or a one night whore?

The Innocent

I'm going to jump forward a number of years now to a period after I left the armed services and became involved with a state prison service. I will get back to my time in the armed forces later in the book.

The prison service is another world, yet ex–servicemen seem to fit into it quite well. Perhaps it's the regimental nature of it all. Who knows?

The bottom line is that when you put a regimented person into a prison full of murderers, rapists, thieves and general low-lives, who don't give a shit about anything, you, more often than not, end up in an explosive situation.

I have survived my share of riots and one-on-one situations over the years and the one thing that sticks out is the fact that the crims seem to respect you if they know you've done the 'hard yards' and, after a while, you get to know them and what makes them tick.

The one universal thing they all have in common is the fact that they are all innocent. That's right, innocent. Just ask them. It's always someone else's fault.

Victim Status

It's easy to get off the hook — get a 'psych' to take a quick look
He'll do his best to rate us — by declaring victim status

Don't get scared once you've been caught
— get a lawyer to submit a report
He won't let anyone bait us — by pronouncing victim status

Now you can do what you want to do — take drugs — be a loser too
We don't care who really hates us — 'cos we've got victim status

Wound, maim and steal — kill while scoring a deal
No one will try to rake us — we've got victim status

Get booked for driving irrationally — claim foreign nationality
The papers might try to bake this — but we've got victim status

Get busted for doing a vault — who cares — wasn't our fault
The police might try to make us — but we've got victim status

Addictive personality — no time for rationality
Society might try to rate us — too late — victim status

Our business fails – excess — we call it negative success
The business world might hate us — but we've got victim status

Take no blame for doing wrong — just sit back — it won't take long
Someone will come to save us — by declaring victim status

We used to take the blame — for stupidity as it came
How will history rate us — for inventing victim status?

Enjoy it

John Lennon once said, 'Life is what happens to you while you're busy making other plans'. How right he was.

We sometimes get that engrossed in what we're doing that we forget the fact that we are living.

It doesn't matter whether you are incarcerated, raising children, playing sports or just doing nothing. We all are doing the same thing. We just don't know how to enjoy it.

Some

Some people walk, some people run
Some don't do anything — to some it's just fun

Some people lose and some people win
Some do it easy while others just cringe

Some just accept it while some want to fight
Some want to hide away like thieves in the night

Some want to work and some want to play
Some wish it was over — some want delay

Some won't accept it and some want to grow
Some want to prosper from the seeds that they've sowed

Some will find riches — some will stay poor
Some will work hard to open those doors

Some will remember — some will forget
Some with kind fondness — some with regret

Some will have hard times and some people won't
Some will find love while some hope they don't

Some will just let it simply pass them by
It's as sure as the blue that colours our sky

Some will enjoy it with every breath
Some won't be happy until they find death

Some won't think it's worth trouble and strife
But we all must experience this thing we call life

Zoos

As a person who grew up in the country and one who has travelled the world quite a bit, I guess I'm as guilty as any of us for taking for granted what nature has to offer 'out there'.

We see nature's wonders every day, but we are usually so consumed by what we are doing that everything else becomes superfluous.

During my time in the services I was fortunate enough to see creatures in their natural habitat and, at the time, paid scant attention to what I was looking at.

Now that I'm older and wiser, although the latter is questionable, I can sit back and reflect on the wonderful things I experienced and realise, in reflection, just how little attention I paid to them at the time.

I think that perhaps we might all be guilty of taking nature for granted at one time or other which is kind of silly when you understand that we are all a part of it.

Gaze In Wonder

We take for granted, nature's gifts
We seem to have forgotten
What gave us a lift

Like soaring eagles up high in the sky
A sight so regal with a deadly eye

When we were younger we looked in awe
And gazed in wonder at the things we saw

Like desert pythons sliding through the plains
Or the wildest brumbies with wind-blown manes

But now we're older and don't seem to care
About the things nature has 'out there'

Like the majestic dolphin — a creature so true
That rules the waves of the ocean blue

We get so busy day to day
To see wild creatures we have to pay

But to see the beauty of a hive of bees
With enough power to bring a man to his knees

Or the elegant beauty of a bounding 'roo
Who roams the country with plenty to do

To see the miracle nature has on show
Is really quite simple and don't cost much dough
Just get off your bums — get out of your chairs
And gaze in wonder at what's 'out there'

The Parent Trap

When you grow up and become a parent, you certainly begin to understand the problems associated with that particular job. It isn't easy to say the least.

Once your children become old enough to leave home and make their own way, you begin to relax a little and get on with reshaping your own life. Usually this results in a happy ending, but not always.

A friend of mine and his wife managed to convince their teenage boys that living at home and saving money for the future was the way to go.

At first the boys resisted this but, in the end, begrudgingly agreed to try it.

The parents thought they had won a major victory over the boys but they didn't realise they'd only won the war, the battle was yet to begin.

Upstairs/Downstairs

Once upon a time in a building oh so near
The top was full of grime whilst downstairs was always clear
It seems that if you lived 'on top' you didn't have to care
You'd have to follow what they both did 'down there'

Don't wash up all your dishes and never put them away
Don't worry 'bout those that follow — it's not your job anyway
If you wash your hands like others — you won't leave stains on doors
And don't worry about sweeping the crumbs you've left on floors

Downstairs seems too stable for your feral atmosphere
Just leave food scraps on the table — you don't wipe them away up
here And never wipe the stove top — mother will take care of that
Don't worry 'bout clothes and old socks — just leave them all to stack

Your rooms are really quite dismal — there is no hit or miss
And there'll never be a refusal — you can rest assured of this
To let it lay — just leave it — yes for those who follow
And even if they don't show up — it will still be there tomorrow

You give no thought to anyone — of that I can truly say
And when all is said and done — you don't care any way
You don't respect each other — and you don't even wonder why
And really why should you bother — you like to live in sties

While downstairs it's quite evident — the respect that is on show
The cleanliness and hygiene that's there for those who know
That to clean up after yourself doesn't really take too much
And the fact that it's returned in find — clean pots and pans to touch

Although we love those who live upstairs — a love we really mean
If you want to live without a care — don't want to keep things clean
Please take this message from us two — the most serious we can give
Pack your bags without further ado — and find somewhere else to live

The Price You Pay

I worked for fourteen years in the armed forces and for fourteen years with the Department of Correctional Services.

As I have already said, I will cover my time in the services later on in the book. Apart from 'Victim Status' I don't recall much about my time in corrections that is repeatable in this book. Perhaps that may come out in the future.

After leaving corrections, I commenced a ten-year run with my companies and was reasonably successful at what I did to the point where other business owners would come and see me to see if I could assist them with their ailing businesses.

I would often listen to them telling me what was required to succeed in business and the sacrifices you had to make.

How many of you know or have known a person who works twenty-four hours a day, seven days a week? I think we all know at least one.

Some might think these people are successful at what they do, but has anyone ever asked the price they had to pay?

I wonder if the 24/7s even know.

Redemption

Look at achievers — look at what they've done
Think of all the battles they have fought and won
Think of all the mountains they have had to climb
Just to ensure that goals were reached on time

They seem to do things with consummate ease
They stroll through problems — just like a breeze
With little pressure to burden them down
You'd think they're the best — doing the rounds

You might have been there — reached the top
Or almost got there — before you stopped
So maybe you know — the truth of the day
They all achieve — but then they pay

Most were married — with a family
That was stripped away, like bark from a tree
The family love that drifts away
Because of the hours they worked every day

They continue to work without any rest
In dreams of reaching their greatest success
They fail to know or understand
That they've sold their souls — to a business plan

And when it's over — when their time is done
Do they understand — what they had is gone?
To obtain success is a hell of a ride
But the price you pay won't redeem your pride

So look for redemption before it's too late
Or find a balance at any rate
Just trim the work load, trim the need
Give time to others — then you'll succeed

A Night Out

A friend of mine was telling me that she was planning a night out on the town with a group of her friends and that she was feeling quite apprehensive about it, given the fact that muggings, rapes and assaults were on the increase.

In fact, she was almost dreading the approaching evening.

They were planning on going into the city and, for a country girl who hadn't visited the city very much, this evil, dark, concrete world was full of shadows.

Social Confusion

The evening started well enough — with a group of friends
With drinking and the other stuff — you wished it wouldn't end
A night with so much innocence — a girls' night on the town
But you lost all your competence — by sculling every round

You started out so brightly — like sunlight in the park
But rightly or wrongly — it changes after dark
Through social confusion you are parted from your friends
And like an optical illusion — nice boys want you to bend

The boys are now pestering you — they won't leave you alone
You figure out just what to do — you'll catch a taxi home
You stagger from the venue — running through the city
But after hours — no taxis cruise — isn't it a pity

Now you move along the street — trying not to stray
You hear the sound of running feet — you wish they'd go away
The streets are all deserted now — except for those that follow
But you've got to make it home somehow — and start again tomorrow

You feel they're almost on you — you can't call for assistance
It seems there's nothing you can do — they come with such
persistence Turn down an alley way in the dead of night
Go this-a-way or that-a-way in a state of fright

Beware of the danger that leaps from every bend
Don't talk to any strangers — you wish this night would end
The danger that follows you — coming from the rear
Is heightened by what's in front of you — a darkness full of fear

From somewhere, in that darkened street reaches out a hand
And clamps itself around your neck — you find it hard to stand
The hand has a vice-like grip and is joined by those that follow
They claw at your clothes that rip — you find it hard to swallow

You waken from that frightening dream — you're under no illusion
You're better off at home it seems — you don't need social confusion

True Blue

When I was building my company, I was fortunate enough to have employed a man from central New South Wales who was quiet and unassuming in manner and industrious and loyal in his work ethic.

He worked hard all his life and, although never receiving a decent education, was very good at anything he turned his hand to. No job seemed too arduous for him.

He'd just ask you what you wanted done and then complete the task with minimum fuss.

A Country Boy

Born to a poor home in a simple time
Where hunting and fishing replaced matters of the mind
Schooling took a back seat — no time for education
His days were filled with things to do — working on the station

Quiet and unassuming, he went about his tasks
And whether he was hungry — no one seemed to ask
Not that it bothered him — he had a job to do
All throughout his childhood and as an adult too

Coming from that background, he took what came along
From shearing sheep to picking fruit — it always made him strong
He worked the land for all his life from east and to the west
From north and south they'd hire him knowing they had the best

All day long he'd work the land — working as he must
The long, hard days with little sleep from dawn right through to dusk
And with the blisters and the breaks, he never once complained
He seemed to be impervious to that barrier known as pain

Now he's in his fifties and still working just as hard
From ploughing fields, milking cows, to mustering in the yard
The weathered skin, the sun burned brow, the worn and calloused hands
Make you wonder just how much more of this his body
can actually stand

But when you sit down and talk to him of matters of the past
He takes a sigh, a deep long breath and finally says at last,
'I'm lucky when I think about the times that I have had
At least I never had to work as hard as dear old dad.'

Learning

You're never too old to learn.

I have enjoyed the highs and lows of owning my own business and the one thing I have learned is that, the day you lose the ability to learn, you lose everything.

In 'Redemption' I wrote about people who would sacrifice everything for their business. Some work that hard that they actually believe that their business would fall apart if they weren't 'holding the strings'.

The fact is that they have not learned to share their lives with their loved ones, friends or family.

And they definitely haven't learned that, at the end of the day, there is a price to pay.

Bulletproof

You work so hard for all your life
With nary a thought of trouble and strife
You see your business go through the roof
You feel at times that you're bulletproof

People want you — you're the talk of the town
They know you'll never let them down
You're forever hearing the telephone ring
You feel you could take on everything

You really enjoy these heady days
You take on the world in many ways
You're oh, so glad that you took this route
It certainly helps when you're bulletproof

You get so busy that you miss the signs
That you could be headed for harder times
The warning signs have always been there
But while things worked you just didn't care

Then times get tough and there's no way out
And all your life is surrounded by doubt
You often worry if you're the only one
To work so hard before things went wrong

But if that's all you think your mind is rented
Better stop being so self-centred
Attack the positives — get off the floor
Use your talent to open some doors

Use your mind and all of your cards
To understand — that it's not too hard
We've all been there — you wanted the scoop?
All at once felt bulletproof

Never Forget

I recently asked an elderly friend of mine the secret behind his long and happy marriage. He told me that he first saw his wife at an adventure park and instantly fell in love.

His secret is that he still looks at her now like he did then.

Chain Reaction

It's amazing what happens when you take a chance
It just may change your circumstance
Like walking through an adventure park
When you see a sight that causes a spark

You never know what happens these days
Even lying on grass by a winding maze
When just up ahead — sitting on rocks
You see a wondrous sight by the flying fox

You've rarely seen a lady so fair
With grace and poise and long flowing hair
You're certainly glad you found this attraction
What you need right now is a chain reaction

Can you walk right up — be so bold
To ask her name or a hand to hold
But deep down inside is this fear of rejection
What you're looking for is a hero injection

And just when you think of something to say
You look up ahead, she's walking your way
You're scared and worried that you'll look a clown
When she walks straight up and sits right down

You look in her eyes and she into yours
And like tidal rivers, the pressure pours
It's easy to talk, there's a common bond
And with some work you'll both grow strong

But always remember that wondrous sight
And always hold her in that same bright light
And never forget that first attraction
That led you both to a chain reaction

Love Story

I have previously written about a friend of mine who was headed for a girls' night out on the town. That same girl, recently separated from her husband, embraced her new life as a single girl and had a lot of fun 'playing the field'.

But it wasn't all fun. She would sometimes call me, crying about the guys she thought she loved and how they had let her down. I guess this gives strength to the old adage – 'There's no gain without pain'.

Words On the Wind

So many times, you spoke of your love
As God is your witness from skies up above
Then they take flight — an original sin
Like thieves in the night — just words on the wind

You try to give all that you can
Make someone happy — make it a plan
But you can't get it right — seems nobody wins
Yes, try as you might — it's just words on the wind

Give your heart and all that it holds
This time be true with all of your soul
Just ease some pain — at least begin
But once again it's just words on the wind

Try to commit to someone new
But remember these words — to thine own self be true
Yet as leaves from a tree are thrown in a spin
You just can't see — it's words on the wind

Perhaps you haven't met the right one
The one who'll stop you — bring you undone
Who'll be beside you and leave with a grin
And then no more — words on the wind

Cruising The Murray

There is probably nothing more relaxing than cruising the River Murray on a houseboat. The river offers solitude, peace and rest and more than a few colourful characters. In this bit, you will meet David and Patsy Bean who own a river boat cruise business in Murray Bridge, SA (M.V. Barrungal) and both enjoy a good wine.

You will also meet David and Di Hartman who used to own the Swan Reach Hotel. They always welcomed you with a nice cool glass of ale.

River Ramble

From its pear-like wedge where the cormorants sing
From its tiny mouth where only sand gets in
You cruise the lakes where the cormorants sang
And stop for a beer in the town of Milang

Then you sail the lake and look for a gap
The River Murray — it's on the map
Past large gum trees that must weigh a ton
Then stop for a beer in Wellington

From there you see the willows grow
Put there to ebb a mighty flow
And just when you think they will never end
You stop for a beer in Tailem Bend

Now you commence a very long run
Past sloping hills and tall red gums
The land around seems 'ridgy didge'
So you stop for a beer in Murray Bridge

You like the town and stay for a time
With David and Patsy you share some wine
You cruise there while your motor hums
And stop for a beer in old Mannum

The river now winds 'round every bend
It seems at times it will never end
And just when you think it will sap your will
You stop for beer, you're in Bow Hill

Past Nildottie where the red cliffs start
The sights and sounds they fill your heart
Past the punt where there is no beach
You stop for a beer at the pub in Swan Reach

It's great to sit on the cliffs so high
And share a beer with David and Di
But you have to leave before the sun goes down
And stop for a beer in old Blanchetown

You follow the cliffs with the sun at your back
And dream of owning a riverside shack
To sit and watch where the rivers once ran
So you stop for a beer in historic Morgan

To make the pubs has tested your will
But not half as much as falling downhill
Climbing hills to pubs isn't going so well
So you stop for a beer in a town called Cadell

From there it's just a bit of a hop
You're almost there — you'd better not stop
You feel like you're running wild and free
So you stop for a beer in Waikerie

Then you head for the nearest border
Through Settlers Bend to Overland Corner
You seem to have forgotten the time it took
So you stop for a beer in a town called Moorook

And after a while you set off again
And try not to go to from whence you came
And then to reward a job well done
You stop for a beer — you're in Loxton

You're starting to get a bit weary by now
But you've got to make it through somehow
You've got the equivalent of Bali Belli
You stop for a beer in a town called Berri

With bloodshot eyes, you greet the dawn
Your stomach hurts from coloured yawns
You're nearly there — don't think or linger
Just stop for a beer in good old Paringa

Your eyes are red — your stomach's a knot
Your almost there — better not stop
Just take it all as a bit of a lark
And stop for a beer in the Port of Renmark

Now once your there you turn around
And once again, you're homeward bound
You're turning south to take the gamble
On surviving another river ramble

Just A Thought

I have been fortunate in that I have been able to cruise the entire length of the River Murray in both South Australia and Victoria and one of the best things about the river is the diverse characters you meet on your travels.

I was watching a bloke in a tinny using a pole to push himself along just out of Echuca in Victoria.

I yelled 'hello' to him and asked him if he could remember when the river was that low, that you had to use a pole to move along it.

He told me that the river was as low as he had ever seen it, as he leant against the pole to move further along. So I asked him why he didn't just walk across the river instead of using a pole.

He replied, 'Yabby holes, need to be on the water to find them.'

With that he again leant against the pole to get leverage, but this time the pole kept going down which ended with him doing a somersault into the water.

When he surfaced, he yelled, 'See what I mean — I'd have missed that hole if I didn't have the pole!'

Leading the Way

I have always believed that 'If it has to be – it's up to me' and with this in mind I have always admired people who have broken new ground whether it be in commerce, sport, education or any other field of endeavour.

Boundary Rider

Leaving school — leaving home — time to make your way
You begin your life — wanting to roam
Looking forward to a new day

You're not hemmed in, the world is yours — you are the decider
You vow and declare, no matter what the score
You won't be a boundary rider

'Cos they're fenced in by rules and codes administered by the boss
Some sit there in wigs and robes
And simply can't see the loss

Some work roads and some work banks — working to a plan
They work through life without much thanks
Doing the best they can

The same old job for fifty years — always in the pink
They do their best to please their peers
Never daring to think

They're stuck there in their insular world thinking,
'Oh, what might have been'
If they took a chance — every boy and girl
The sights they could have seen

They've never jumped in or took the plunge — on a daily grind they strive
They just got scared and started to run
Life's too shallow to dive

So dare to be different — pave your own way — you be the decider
Knock down the fences and have your say
Don't be a boundary rider

Dreaming

Met up with an old mate of mine who had always been a devout bachelor and bushie. No women for him. No sirree.

He reckoned they were nothing but trouble and, besides, they were useless in the bush and just messed up your life.

My, how time changes things.

When I caught up with him, he looked tired and worn-out, so I asked him what was wrong.

He told me that he hadn't been sleeping very well for the past couple of weeks because his pillow had gone walkabout.

He went on to tell me that he met a woman some time back and, despite himself, he fell in love and now he had gotten so used to holding her every night he found it difficult to sleep when she was visiting family and such.

Pillows

No matter where I wander
No matter where I roam
My thoughts are never far away
Far away from home

Not to have you near me
My heart weeps like a willow
I find myself alone at night
Holding onto pillows

I love to hold you close to me
To feel your body near
To lay beside you every night
And whisper in your ear

I miss the little things with you
The things you do and say
It fills my heart with sadness
When I'm far away

You've filled my heart with gladness
Like a sail when it billows
I find myself holding you
When I'm holding pillows

From the Heart

When thinking of my old mate I guess that, sooner or later, someone is going to get into your heart. It's unavoidable.

But if you haven't loved for quite some time, the thought of attaching yourself to someone must be scary.

To me, if I was to meet that special someone, it would have to be about sharing and respecting each other.

Questions

If I walk with you — will you walk with me?
If I talk to you — will you talk to me?
If I 'be' with you — will you 'be' with me?
If I see for you — will you see for me?
If I share with you — will you share with me?
If I care for you — will you care for me?
If I lay with you — will you lay with me?
If I pray for you — will you pray for me?
If I give to you — will you give to me?
If I live for you — will you live for me?
If I try for you — will you try for me?
And if I die for you — will you cry for me?

Friends

Most of my friends are married. Some happily, some not.

A common thread among those who have problems with their relationships is the fact that their partners stated that, by marrying them, they wouldn't have to change their lifestyle.

What rubbish!

The mere fact that two people decide to share one life changes both forever.

Perhaps an assertion prior to starting any relationship should be established.

Assertion

I will try to love you as I always have
I will even try harder when things are bad
I will be your companion for as long as I can
As long as you remember — I'm only a man

I need your support and I will give you mine
We can lean on each other almost all the time
But there will be times when I will need a break
To spend some time with my own special mates

There'll be times when I'll want to be by myself
So understand — I'm with no one else
For I can be alone with a group of friends
Just to have them near is a means to an end

Every now and then I won't want to talk
I'll sit there quiet or take a walk
Please don't think you've done something wrong
It's these quieter moments that keep me strong

I promise I'll work hard nearly every day
To lay a foundation or pave a way
To make life easier for every one
And I promise I'll never bring work home

Now there is lots more I can add to my traits
But to lay them bare — you'll just have to wait
Through love and friendship we should do well
If we survive as a couple only time will tell

Time will test our patience as it always does
It will try its best to undo our love
But as I have my faults and you have yours
If we know them all — we may endure

For the path we are on is often worn
Till the end of life from the time we're born
It's not often easy to round each bend
For as much as there's love, we must be friends

Life

After a while, every one of us gets to thinking about life and what it means. To most of us, it's a journey that we all must take. To others it's a series of events that lead to an inescapable conclusion.

Doors

A doorbell rings — a magpie sings
The world is suddenly bright
For by your birth you've brought joy
To those that gave you life

From there to teens and in between
The years go quickly by
And before you know it, the world's grown up
Right before your eyes

From days of clover — you know it's over
You can't play games any more
It's time to move on and start your life
To close that childhood door

Now a young man — you do the best you can
To work hard and save your pay
With wife and kids and rising bills
Life gets harder — day to day

And when they've grown and you're all alone
After years of struggling more
You understand – it's part of a plan
To close another door

You've reached mid-life without much strife
You're not worried about the score
Because you've had the courage — the strength of will
To open all life's doors

Now it's colder — you're getting older
You look forward evermore
To taking the step — turning the handle
And opening that final door

Writer's Block

You often hear this term.

I always figured it was a period of time when writers just lost the plot and needed time to rejuvenate.

Experience has taught me that it's a period of time when you write in dribs and drabs instead of pumping words out at a continuous rate.

You just know the flow will return some day – or will it?

Lost The Gift

It's hard to write when you're feeling flat
You search for ideas — try this and that
The inspirations that came so free
Just disappear — it's hard to see

The things that drove you to jot things down
The thoughts that attacked you whilst driving around
The sights that aroused you — that caused a spark
The things that made you write in the dark

You lose the time that it took to write
To use the computer — sit down and type
You get consumed with other things
Get lost in a void where no rhymes ring

Then frustration sets in — it's really quite sad
You seem to forget the gift you had
You know it's there — just hiding away
And you hope like hell it comes back some day

You know it's in you — you know it's there
But try as you might — you just don't dare
To write things down that make some sense
They disappear — become past tense

I know I've tried for over a year
I've searched through wine and over beer
For ideas that could become a poem
I'd form them all — then they'd roam

So now, I hate what I know to be true
I'll never write like I used to do
I've lost the gift — run out of time
I'll never again write down in rhyme

Found It

Once you've lost the gift of being able to write, you feel that it will never come back. Even though you keep writing spasmodically you can't wait for the 'bursts' to come and are glad when they do.

Writing Again

I feel like writing — feel that old flow
But there's so little time before I must go
To settle that itch — write with a splurge
Oh, the confidence that gives me the nerve

I remember clearly the last time it came
And when it left I thought — never again
Of course, I'd remember the gift that I had
And write spasmodically — in dribs and drabs

Oh, for the days when each verse would fly
The hours that ticked as time went by
The feeling you had at the end of each rhyme
It didn't matter that you'd lost all that time

I just can't wait to write that first verse
With the feeling back I know it won't hurt
Oh, for the joy of writing once more
And then I hear a knock upon my door

My friends come in — it's time to go
We'll have to leave or we'll miss the show
Now I've forgotten what I wanted to write
Perhaps I'll remember during the night

That evening we all had a wonderful time
And still I can't remember what I wanted to rhyme
So you'll have to wait for another look
To see if I remember keep reading this book

Warning Signs

Writing, to me, has always been just a hobby.

It's a hobby I have only shared with a few very close friends. Those friends, over the years, have encouraged me to keep on writing and to eventually publish a book. The writing part I have no problem with because I actually enjoy it and find it easy to do as ideas just seem to flow from every direction. Publishing a book is something else entirely.

A book should have a beginning, a middle and an end, with a strong storyline to hold it all together. What you have just read doesn't have any of these qualities. It is just a collection of observations that I have taken the liberty to put down on paper, as I find it easier to express my feelings through the written word rather than orally. Besides, it was never my intention to publish anything that I have written. It was merely my way of expressing my feelings to my friends. An outlet, if you like.

In each poem, I have mostly written about other people and what I see in them or what I see that could help them whether that is in their business life, personal dealings or private matters. At no stage, other than the obvious ones, did I think I was writing about myself.

It's funny how you're the last one to see what is right in front of you.

My friends started to notice a change in me a few years ago. Apparently, I became distant, non-communicative, drinking more etc. They even tried to warn me that they thought something was wrong by asking if I was alright, how the business was going, was my private life okay etc. Without knowing it, I was in a state of denial and fobbed off their well-meaning enquiries with a 'she'll be right' attitude.

I should have listened. As I've said the warning signs were already in place. They were hidden inside 'Redemption', 'Bulletproof' and 'Doors'. I just didn't see them.

The truth is that, at the time, my business was falling apart; my private life was a mess and I was totally lost with no idea of what was happening to me or why.

I was shaking every day for no reason, crying every night for no reason, scared to walk into my office, scared to face my friends and hiding in corners when the telephone rang. Instead of talking to my friends about it or seeking medical help, I jumped into a deep, dark hole where, to me, there seemed to be only one way out.

The Fight

Depression is like a good sucker punch.

You don't see it coming.

In fact, you could have it for years before it hits you.

It can happen to anyone. It could be hiding within you right now just lacing up its gloves, getting ready to strike. The first few blows might be subtle. In fact, you mightn't even notice them. After all, They're just left jabs.

You start to spend less time at work — too tired?

Less time with family and friends — rather be alone?

Sleeping less — restless?

Then you receive a few right crosses.

Drinking more — helps you sleep?

Reclusive — don't need anyone?

Argumentative — they don't understand?

Short tempered — just leave me alone.

Now you don't understand what's happening to you and you duck for cover. Not a good move. Upper cuts.
Nightmares — memories of the past.
Crying at night — why?
Unable to face work — too scared?
Unable to talk to any one — embarrassed?
Drinking binges — every day.
Anger — constant.
Shaking — continual.

Even at this stage of the fight, you may not realise that you are suffering depression. It takes time. Sucker punch.
Loss of interest — in everything.
Feelings — gone.
Understanding — gone.
Relationships — gone.
Self-worth — gone.
Value of life — gone.
Everything — gone.

One of the sad things about this fight is that it has been going on inside you for years. You just didn't know it. The other sad fact is that all of the above is only round one. It is but a small part of the greater picture that is known as Post Traumatic Stress Disorder (PTSD).

The following verses do not paint a pretty picture but they do convey the truth about what you can expect when going through the turmoil of depression and PTSD and, hopefully, show you that there is a light at the end of the tunnel.

Eulogy

I once attended a funeral where I listened to someone giving a eulogy for his recently departed friend and, at the time, I thought that what he was saying seemed inadequate for the occasion.

So I thought it might be a good idea to write my own eulogy. Not to be morbid, but more as a celebration of my life and the great friends I have made along the way.

Family and even good friends certainly make up a greater part of our lives and, at the end of the day, they are the ones we owe our lives to.

Close the Windows

Close the windows and lock the doors
Shut the gate forever more
Turn your backs and leave my place
And leave me with a smile on your face

Tell my friends that I loved them all
Throughout my life, we had a ball
I'll miss them now that my time has come
I held them dear — each and every one

Tell my family — I did the best I could
Tell them all that it's understood
That they each loved me in their own way
And that love is returned on my very last day

Now as I leave, I want you all to know
That without you all — there was no glow
So think of me when you're in the sun
And shine for me — when all is done

There's one last favour I will ask of you
Just one more thing I want you all to do
Close my windows and lock my doors
And simply say, 'He's not here anymore.'

Right Crosses & Upper Cuts

Sometimes, without knowing it, you are spinning out of control and you try desperately for something to hang onto.

When there is nothing to hold onto, you feel yourself dropping into a dark place where no one should go. The headaches won't stop. The nightmares keep you awake all night to the point where you just sit there crying. The daylight hours bring on the shakes. You just want it all to stop.

You even get to the point of planning a way to making it all stop. You even know when and where you're going to do it.

Then something tells you to make one last cry for help.

Demons

There's a calmness when it hits you — hits you from the blue
I've thought about it for quite some time
I know what I must do

I know just where I'll stand my last — without looking to the past
Just one more step without much thought
I hope the end comes fast

I wonder how I got here — reaching more than I could bear
What leads me to that final step?
Where I really just don't care

I used to handle everything — all that life could bring
But something snapped — I don't know what
But something from within

For several months, I've fought it — trying with all my might
To justify what's going on
In mind — it's just not right

I've had some days when all was well — as crystal as a bell
Then something would happen — a minor thing
And all would turn to hell

I've often thought of suicide — a way to end the ride
To drag me from that bottomless pit
Where there's nowhere left to hide

I'm tired of always having to fight the demons from within
I've lost my loves and businesses
I know I just can't win

So there's a calmness when it hits you — hits you from the blue
Yes, I've thought about it for quite some time
Now I know what I must do

Suckerpunch

After your last attempt to reach for hope, despair and hopelessness seem to take over your whole being. You just can't see a way out.

You don't stop and think about the impact of what you are about to do will have on your friends and family. In fact, you become single-minded. You become so determined to end it all that you develop a tunnel vision and nothing on this earth will stop you.

Once you have reached this stage you don't threaten to do it, you don't drop hints of what you might be thinking of doing, you just do it. End of argument.

You could be spending time with your best friends or closest family members and they wouldn't have a clue. You have, rightly or wrongly, made your decision.

I have always been a bit of a loner and never really let anyone get too close to me. Attempting to take my own life certainly changed all that. After spending some days in a hypobaric chamber to get rid of the carbon monoxide that had filled my body and an equal number of days in a coma, I awoke to an understanding that to end it all was not the answer.

I awoke in time to start the next phase of my life; a phase that would lead me to explore the person that is me.

Perdition

The road to perdition is a path well-worn
By those in limbo, whose lives are torn
They've tried for assistance, even carried the cross
But it all became pointless when their souls got lost

So they reach a stage where there is no doubt
That the only way out is to turn the lights out
To turn those lights out is a vision so clear
And it's even peaceful when the end is near

But if you survive, though your heart's a whimper
You find with help that life's much simpler
Your friends and family gather oh so near
And even some friends you haven't seen for years

They pull together doing all they can
To help you out with a lifetime plan
They try to help you with love and rest
And try to convince you that you don't need death

I know, I've been there — no hit or miss
I even enjoyed stepping into the abyss
But I failed in my mission — got found too soon
So I just got angry and planned my next move

But they put me in hospital under lock and key
And tried to help me but they just couldn't see
That I'd made my mind up to round that bend
And bring my misery to a final end

Then family and friends gathered from near and far
Some by plane and others by car
They never questioned the path I chose
They just let me know that they'd always be close

Then my brother and sister, with a calming air
Said not to worry they'd take care of my affairs
My mother didn't want my life to end
And she was backed up by all of my friends

I've lived alone nearly all my life
And always got scared of taking a wife
I've only had time for fellow vets
And never cared for all the rest

But ever since I've crossed death's door
I've discovered that life holds so much more
There's family and friends that'll help you through
And stand beside you no matter what you do

And although they did nearly all they could
I have told them all — I'm not out of the woods
For dark thoughts circle around in my head
But at least they've showed me there's a light up ahead

Perhaps I'll get there or maybe I won't
Some want to be there while others don't
But with friends and family I might get well
To see if l make it — only time will tell

Just A Thought

When I came out of my coma, after almost doing myself in, I was surprised to see all my family had gathered around me to offer all the support they could.

Most people who suffer depression have suffered it for years without knowing it. I was no different. I had always considered my family a little dysfunctional, as none of them had the same work ethic that I possessed and all of them seemed quite happy with their lot in life.

I was different in that I always strived to be the best at any endeavour I undertook. Even if it meant that I worked 24/7. I honestly thought that success was the way to happiness. How wrong I was.

At this early stage of my rehabilitation, I could see that my family had always been there for me. I wasn't there for them when they needed me. This is where the realization of the fact that you are self-centred starts to set in.

I can now see that it was the first step towards understanding exactly who I was and where I wanted to be. All I needed was a safe haven to go 'cold turkey' in terms of facing up to myself.

Safe Haven

After being released from intensive care I was transferred to Ward 17 at Daw Park Repatriation Hospital in Adelaide, South Australia.

Ward 17 looks after returned servicemen and specialises in Post-Traumatic Stress Disorders or PTSD and its associated illnesses such as depression, anxiety, panic attacks, etc.

This was where I discovered that I wasn't crazy – I actually had an illness that could be treated.

I spent a total of ten weeks in Ward 17 where I received a good grounding on the fundamentals of what was wrong with me and a good understanding that my road to recovery could take years.

The doctors and staff of Ward 17 are second to none and go out of their way to let you know that they actually care for you and want you to feel safe at all times.

Daw Park

Don't open the door — don't be so dense
Don't walk down the drive — don't climb the fence
If you open the door — you might go outside
If you walk down the drive — there's nowhere to hide

For once you're 'out there' you lose control
You find yourself falling with nothing to hold
You'll run off the rails which is nothing new
You might hurt someone — who knows what you'll do

You have to understand you've been ill for a while
With pain and confusion there's no reason to smile
You might get angry and give everyone hell
When all along it's you that's not well

Ever wonder why you're always alone?
Or had all sorts of trouble keeping a home
Have you ever wondered why you've held back the tears?
Is there a realisation you've been like this for years?

For years you thought there was nothing wrong
When all of a sudden all you had is gone
You blame yourself when it all falls apart
And begin to question — when did it start?

You reach the depths where no one should go
You hide from your friends — you don't want them to know
You struggle and fight to get rid of the doubt
And in your mind you see no way out

But there is an answer — professional help
They know what you've gone through and how you've felt
They know how to treat you — get you back on track
And try to teach you why you're feeling so flat

There's no guarantees — you might need it some more
But at least they'll always open the doors
So if you're lost — can't see through the dark
There is a safe haven here at Daw Park

Roller-Coaster

Once you arrive in hospital you get into a false sense of security that all will be right, but the truth is that being admitted is only the first step on the roller-coaster ride that leads to recovery.

With PTSD you have days when everything is crystal clear, whilst other days are cloudy and confusing. You find yourself questioning your past, worrying about your future, crying for those you've hurt along the way and forever searching for answers.

In the early stages there is more self — doubt than confidence.

Daylight

Daylight, daylight where can you be?
Though the sun's shining bright — you can't see me
I'm paper thin with no real substance
Leading a life that made no sense

Daylight, daylight why did you hide?
I look for you each day with a weathered eye
I've led a life less than true don't you see
Help me to find the man within me

Daylight, daylight where are you now?
I need you to help me make it through somehow
The people I've hurt without compunction
My life has left a trail of destruction

Daylight, daylight why did you leave?
I suppose you didn't like what you saw in me
I see it now and I want to explore
To find who I am — at least open the door

Daylight, daylight is there a reward?
I can't go back and I can't go forward
To go ahead I'll learn all I can
To make myself a better man

Daylight, daylight I hope it will end
I'd dearly love to see you again
I dread to take a backward step
And fear that awkward forward trek

Daylight, daylight will you shine once more
Deliver your light right to my door
Sew back my life like a doctor's suture
'Cos I'm scared of the past — not sure of the future

Anger

The constant headaches, confusion, shaking and insecurity you experience whilst suffering depression leaves you with a very short fuse and anger becomes part of your everyday life.

Sometimes you think that the only way that you are not going to hurt someone is to isolate yourself.

Do Not Disturb

Don't disturb me now — I'm not feeling quite right
To disturb me now might lead to a fight
I need to be alone to figure things out
So leave me be — 'til I turn things about

Don't ask me why I'm feeling this way
Or why it happens — I just can't say
For things get scrambled inside my head
And where they'll lead me I really dread

I've been like this for some time now
I just get angry for no reason somehow
It's not just you — it's everyone
I'm better off if I'm left alone

It's not every day for goodness sake
It's only on days when I begin to shake
My head starts spinning out of control
I feel myself falling with nothing to hold

An innocent comment might set me off
And I won't back down 'til I'm on top
For I just black out — don't know what I'll do
And there's a very real chance that I might hurt you

I'm getting help and trying to win
And with this help I won't give in
But until I'm there — beware the danger
We might be friends — but you could be a stranger

On the odd days when you see me alone
And staying away from every one
Don't disturb then — I won't be feeling quite right
To disturb me then could lead to a fight

Family

I've never been close to my family. I have thought that they were all a little bit dysfunctional. Even during childhood, I found it difficult to associate with my brothers and sisters. It's a feeling I held throughout most of my adult life.

We have very rarely communicated with each other and we're lucky if we gathered as a family once every five or six years. Even then, there was usually one member of the family missing.

After a while, I had delusions of grandeur that I was the only one that was on the right track in terms of knowing what family love was all about.

Then, after I 'crashed', I awoke from my coma to find the whole family gathered around me.

Left Of Centre

For years, you thought they were left of centre
Dysfunctional without love to render
They all left home when they came of age
And carried on living, each their own way

Some would wander and start to roam
While others were happy to make a home
You wouldn't see each other for a year or more
And there'd only be Mum home when you walked through the door

She'd tell you of the family's plight
Each brother and sister — into the night
She wishes they'd all turned out like you
But they seemed to find trouble no matter what they'd do

And on those occasions when everyone's there
Yes those occasions that are quite rare
They seemed like strangers you don't quite know
And after a while, you can't wait to go

They've mostly been married maybe once or twice
And been divorced after paying the price
You think they can't do anything well
Each brother and sister — who can tell

Then something happens, you fall into a hole
And they stand beside you — fulfilling a role
They gather around you which is oh, so rare
And you understand that they really do care

They rally together like a well-trained team
And can't do enough to mend the seams
They tell you how they've always been tight
Just waiting for you to come home one night

They all say they love you and you understand
This really is a tight knit clan
For years the love, they've tried to render
When all along — you were left of centre

Self Doubt

The path to recovery from PTSD and depression is a very, very rough one. There is no easy way. You find yourself continually fighting thoughts of suicide, worthlessness, confusion and self-doubt to mention a few.

These thoughts are coupled with moments of clarity when you know the answers but just can't make them happen.

Tug Of War

Sometimes I think my life's a tug of war
I feel I've lost — feel I know the score
There are people around you who really care
Tell them about it — make them aware

I get depressed — feel my life's a bore
feel at times like a worthless whore
Find something to do that might assist
Get out of the gutter — who knows what you've missed?

Sometimes I'm tempted to go out the door
Walk out on life — exist no more
Remember your family and all of your friends
And all you'd hurt if your life should end

But dreams come back where I'm lost evermore
No fruit in the future for me I'm sure
Dreams are but dreams that fade with the night
And if you are strong, there is fruit within sight

I feel no love — nothing to adore
There's a wall around me — a useless bore
The walls around you will come crashing down
And there's always someone waiting to be found

There are things in life that I abhor
They set me off — get lost once more
We all have hates and that's a fact
Just step aside — avoid the traps

My mind gets lost — I'm never sure
To live or die — don't care anymore
The tug of war in minds and hearts
Cannot be won before it starts

Troughs

After you've been in hospital for a while, the medication they give you starts to kick in and you start to feel a little bit more comfortable within yourself.

You even let yourself fall into a false sense of security just because you've experienced three or four days where the headaches have disappeared, the shakes have stopped, you're sleeping better and the nightmares have gone.

Yes, you really think you're well and truly on the road to recovery.

Quick Fix

The headaches you had are a thing of the past
They're really gone — gone at last
And those sleepless nights have come to an end
On a good night's sleep you can depend

They bring it home like a lightning bolt
You've been blaming yourself when it's not your fault
You learn to relax — take it all in
And try to come back from where you've been

You'll even sit back — call friends on the 'phone
And start to find your comfort zone
You like to think you're moving ahead
You've let go of the past — come back from the dead

You're eager to learn just what went wrong
To understand what you've said and done
And with their help you can always tell
That with continued counselling you'll soon get well

Medication seems to ease the pain
You look forward to living life again
You think you've made all the pieces fit
But deep down you know there is no quick fix

For late one night without a call
The past will come back and open the door
Then all those pieces fall apart again
And you're reverted back to a life of pain

Yes all of a sudden the headaches come
And the sleepless nights bring you undone
The nightmares that hurt you cut to the core
And you feel yourself slipping back once more

You feel the anger building up inside
And other feelings you just can't hide
You thought you had the answers — knew all the tricks
When all along there was no quick fix

So you have to learn and understand
To deal with what's happening — set a plan

Listen to others who know the score
And let them help you out once more
You have to know that this could take some time
And could continue into your prime

It may continue for the rest of your days
So you'll have to deal with it in your own safe way
So to stop the dreams and get some sleep
Here's a secret we all should keep

Just gather your thoughts and throw this in the mix
There never was an easy quick fix

Just A Thought

This part is important. There simply is no quick fix.

Depression is something that may take years to get over, if you ever do. The trick is to deal with it. I must admit that when I first got to Daw Park I did not have the faintest idea about it and what it does to you.

With hindsight now in my back pocket, I can tell you that dealing with it is not easy and is definitely not something you can do alone. You need help. At this point in time (July 2008) it has been just over a year and a half since I was admitted to hospital and 15 months since my discharge. Without the help of my friends and family I can honestly say that I wouldn't be here today. They have all been fantastic.

Over what could be a long period of time, there are going to be times when you are by yourself, feeling like you're slipping backwards again and losing control over your emotions. As I have said, there is no quick fix but there is help available.

You could call your friends and talk to them about it or you could ring Beyond Blue and they will, in the first instance, willingly give you support and then direct you to the nearest regional help office or the nearest like-minded support office in your region or city. If you are suffering from depression please remember this.

I know I have used these services in the past and will continue to do so in the future or for as long as it takes.

Meeting Place

Just outside Ward 17 there's a building designed for smokers. Over the years, it has become a place where all the diggers can sit down and get grievances off their chest as well as a place where we can share a joke or two.

It's a place where you can get advice on just about everything.

The Cave

There is a room just outside the ward
Full of souls trying to go forward
They laugh at times at the crudest of jokes
And cough their lungs out from acrid smoke

They try to make light of the situation they're in
And rarely talk about where they've been
Some may get better no matter what it takes
While some need time out — make an escape

This is a place where they can all rant and rave
And in a technical way, it's called 'The Cave'
It can be a place where they're at their best
Or get some shit right off their chests

It can be a place where you're on your own
It can be a place where you're never alone
It can be a place of decadence and vice
And it can be a place where you get good advice

It's a place that really deserves our respect
A haven that helps us clean up our mess
A cavern that clears away darkening clouds
With a sign on the mat 'No dick heads allowed'

Diggers

Conversations in 'The Cave' cover many varied fields, but a common thread in all discussions is the constant battle each digger has to go through just to get what they rightfully deserve.

It's all right for those in the corridors of power to send boys off to war but when these people return from the war, the powerbrokers who sent them there in the first place, aren't in office anymore.

It's then left up to the diggers to beg and fight for their pensions and entitlements by trying to explain themselves to those who sometimes do not even remember the Vietnam War.

I wonder if the ones in power even care about what they have done to these men.

It appears to me that the main concern is about saving the government's money and not looking after those who have put their lives on the line for their country.

Sad, isn't it?

Farm Boy

He worked the fields and sowed the seeds
On his father's hard-earned farm
When his number fell for his country's needs
Time to do some harm

They drilled him hard and taught him well
With him you'd never trifle
With unarmed combat, he'd give you hell
Then they gave to him a rifle

They trained him hard to learn the skill
Each bullet went like thunder
'Don't mess 'round boy — shoot to kill'
Then they sent him off to Canungra

After training there, the authorities claim
Working to a plan
He's ready now to go take aim
In a foreign land

In Vietnam where time began
And life had once stood still
He stood the test just like the rest
And walked away from life's hill

On returning home, he was all alone
And no one really cared
About the times and hardships
He had suffered over there

So he took to the booze and fought the fights
Working from bar to bar
And stayed that way for most of his life
Never the rising star

They taught him well to use the sword
To get through life somehow
What's left is in a psycho ward
Where's that farm boy now?

Recognition

A big part of the recovery process is recognising the warning signs. These signs may come to you via nightmares that continually attack your reasoning.

Failing to recognise the signs is what got me here in the first place.

Recognising them is one thing – fighting back is another.

Long, Black Clouds

They're back again — those long, black clouds
In my head — screaming loud
Telling me to end it all
Warning me to heed their call

They're showing me just what to do
Telling me it'll soon be through
Implying that they won't go away
Until I meet my judgement day

They're warning me — I'll go straight to hell
Telling me — I'll never get well
Scaring me that I'll stay unglued
Unless I do what they want me to

They're telling me it's the only way out
My head hurts so — I could really shout
I tried to join them once — what's done is done
I wish they'd just leave me alone

I want to live — I want my life
But life's so hard when you're forced to fight
Those long, black clouds when they come
I wouldn't wish this fight on any one

But I can't give in — let them play their cards
I have to fight and fight real hard
I must stand up — make myself proud
And rid myself of these long, black clouds

Understanding

Once you start to recognise some of the symptoms, you start to gather an understanding of how and why these things are happening to you. Even though there is medical help through pills and counselling, the bulk of the repair work must be done by the patient.

So recognition and understanding are both steps to recovery that should be pursued by all who suffer PTSD and all its associated illnesses.

Steps

Depression is like descending steps
Spiralling ever downward
Each step is like the very next
Going down but never forward

You never know when it's going to start
That awkward downward trek
But something takes over your head and heart
And you find you're on the steps

When you start to head downhill
Your mind at once is set
Then something seems to sap your will
You take the first few steps

While this goes on you are unaware
Of just how fast it gets
The pace picks up — you just don't care
You're falling down the steps

The funny thing is you can't recognise
What's happening to you
You can't arrange or organise
A rescue plan to do

So you just keep falling — having a bash
Waiting for the wreck
That's bound to happen after the crash
At the bottom of the deck

There are many roads you can take from here
From the bottom of the deck
You could end it all or drown in beer
Or climb back up those steps

Realisation

Self-doubt is something that constantly creeps back into your thoughts. The major doubt is a belief in yourself.

In the early stages, you often find yourself looking into a mirror and not liking what you see. You start to see the faults that you've had quite some time now and realise that there are a number of things you could have done better.

All you need is the ability to conquer your fears.

Fear

It could be about anything
Like failing to show emotion
It could be about everything
Even lack of true devotion

It could be about failing to give
Or lack of patience — having to wait
It could be about the will to live
Or being too scared to cross that gate

It could be about failing to share
Or letting everyone down
Or the feeling of hurting those who care
Letting them go without a sound

It could be about lonely despair
Or the thoughts turning in your mind
It could be just a single nightmare
Or the mess you've left behind

It could be about wanting to hide
Not sharing your life with those you love
It could be about loss of pride
Or perhaps it's nearly all the above

So when it comes down to it
Here's something you don't want to hear
You eventually have to face up to it
And conquer all your fears

This is easier said than done
Fighting demons year by year
For only then the battle's won
Can you conquer all your fears

Hiding

A lot of people who have depression and/or PTSD spend most of their lives in four states of being:

1. Alcoholic

2. Workaholic

3. Suicidal

Or

4. Recovering

I became a workaholic. I became obsessed with spending as much time as I could making sure everything I undertook came off without a hitch.

I remained in this state of being for thirty odd years without really understanding what I was doing. I thought I was driven to prove to people that I was the best person for any job anywhere. This included my business.

What I was actually doing was hiding. Hiding from the past, hiding from my friends and family, hiding from the fact that there was actually something wrong with me and hiding from the fact that I was an alcoholic.

I was hiding behind a wall called work without realising that this wall was about to come crashing down.

Fire In The Belly

You get used to it, hour after hour, day after day
You even thrive on it, working without pay
The ideas seem to grow — greater every year
You've got that creative flow — never any fear

You start with something new, want to watch it grow
There's always plenty to do, to help those seeds you've sowed
You do all you can, the best you can possibly do
To create a business plan, to ensure that it all runs true

You become consumed by it, don't take a holiday
You become controlled by it, controlled in every way
Seven days for sixteen hours, no time for friends or telly
You're even enjoying it — this fire in the belly

You think you're way on top — way on top of the heap
Why would you want this to stop — when you're leading all the sheep?
It's got nothing to do about wealth, its gone way past that
You don't worry about your health — keep that one under your hat

You become obsessed about creating and sometimes become irate
You even avoid debating, concern coming from your mates
You forget your entire family — you treat them less than right
You wish they'd just let you be, so you can work at night

And then you lose control — your tents are not in line
You seem to lose your soul — something's got you from behind
You've worked so hard for years — and watched it turn to jelly
You don't want any more tears — no more fire in the belly

Nightmares

Not too long after I got out of the armed forces, I left my wife and son. I have no idea why I did this for she was and still is a terrific woman whose only crime was to fall in love with the wrong man.

My son has never forgiven me and probably never will. I can't blame him because it took me many, many years to figure out what was going on and I don't expect him to understand the fact that, in my mind, I thought I was doing them a favour by leaving.

They both remain part of my nightmares.

I never knew my grandfather on my father's side. No one ever spoke of him. It seemed that he was the black sheep of the family. After the way our father raised us, his father must have done something pretty horrible to make him blacker than his son.

Whilst I was in hospital, my mother called and I told her of these thoughts that were adding to my confusion. She finally opened up about my grandfather and a whole world of reasoning spread out before me. Things were starting to fall into place.

The Penny

1914 to 1918 the war to end all wars
He fought them in the trenches — he fought them on the shores
He fought for the English — for a foreign cause
But it didn't really matter — No one was keeping score

And when it all was over — when he had survived
He returned home and travelled the whole country wide
He was looking for something that would redeem his pride
And he found it with a woman who would become his bride

Life was pretty happy then — they left a good impression
But things soon came crashing down — with the great recession
Life was so much harder now — choking with compression
And although he didn't know it then
He'd sunken into depression

That's when he started drinking — not talking to anyone
He'd stare for hours at nothing — then the shakes would start to
come His wife would try to talk to him — he'd hit before she'd run
And the violence wasn't exclusive
He'd even beat up on his son

Although scared for most of their lives, they'd never call a cop
For they loved him very dearly and hoped it all would stop
The son joined the army after all the pain he'd copped
And both missed the opportunity — to see the penny drop

1939 to 1945 the years of World War Two
The son was sent overseas — he had a job to do
He fought the war on many fronts — to the shores of Kathmandu
And they didn't send him home again
Until the war was through

Back home with the war tucked safely at the rear
His wife and he raised a son who they proudly held quite near
They lived their lives quite blissfully — no need for any fear
Until the night, he packed his bags
And they sent him to Korea

1950 to 1953 saw the Korean War
And here we go once again — fighting someone else's war
And like before he was dodging bullets on a foreign shore
But it didn't really matter
No one was keeping score

But when he came home — he wasn't the same that went away
He was different somehow — his mannerisms and his casual sway
He'd lost interest in his loving wife and son who wanted to play
And when she was alone at night
She wondered if he'd even stay

That's when he started drinking — not talking to anyone
He'd stare for hours at nothing and the shakes would start to come
His wife would try to talk to him — he'd hit her before she'd run
And the violence wasn't exclusive
He'd beat up on his son

Although scared for most of their lives they'd never called a cop
For they loved him very dearly and hoped it all would stop
The son joined the Navy after all the pain he'd copped
And both missed the opportunity
To see the penny drop

1962 to 1973 the war in Vietnam
Where they kitted him up and sent him off to do the best he can
As in the past to fight someone else's fight in a foreign land
And after his time they said 'Well done'
And sent him home a man

Back home he got real lucky — married and settled down well
Had a son — had it all — even a house that they could sell
He had his own business — could go anywhere — who could tell
Then things went wrong — started to crash
And everything turned to hell

That's when he started drinking — not talking to anyone
He'd stare for hours at nothing and the shakes would start to come
His wife would try to talk to him — he'd tell her to take a run
And his abuse wasn't exclusive
He'd even yell at his own son

He knew he'd soon get violent — thought they'd call a cop
Somewhere deep within himself he wanted it all to stop
History told him of the violence his family had always copped
So he caught the opportunity
He saw the penny drop

Though he loved his wife and family, he knew he had to go
For to stay there with them would take them to a new low
To break that military chain required a fearful blow
And to give your own heart
Is the strongest blow we know

He won't understand why he's done this — won't understand for
years He'll just reach for a Kleenex and wipe away the tears
They become part of his nightmares part of the problems at hand
Until it suddenly hits him
And he finally understands

Now he travels around the land — moving from place to place
And he travels real slowly — after all, he's not in a race
He never stops to worry or take the time from a clock
He's just glad he broke the chains
When he saw the penny drop

Now that he has finally faced those demons from the past
It brings home some of the questions those nightmares used to ask
He finally understands why his family fell apart
It's been happening for many years
It was doomed before the start

The next stage is to deal with all that has been churned
For dealing with the past is something we must learn
When the learning process starts — he'll never want to stop
'Cos he'll always remember the time
He saw the penny drop

They're Good!

All the psychiatrists, doctors, nurses, day-care facilitators and the social worker within Ward 17 are the best at what they do. They are second to none, not because of what they do professionally, but for going that extra yard in relation to the care and advice they provide you.

Everyone who has ever been in Ward 17 knows what I'm talking about. They have all had days when they have 'collapsed' and dived into the feeling of insecurity.

This is where the Ward 17 staff come into their own. They notice when you are down and will quite often walk into your room and ask if they can talk to you. This is when they are at their best.

The Trip

Settle down and rest my friend
On a good night's sleep
You can depend
For just ahead, around the bend
Your troubles will come
To an end

It might take a while to get you there
But the trip's made easy
By those who care
There are many bumps so be aware
Just stay on the road
It'll get you there

There are some deep valleys and some hard hills
And the going gets tough
So take your pills
You may fall over — take some spills
So you have to show
Your strength of will

The road's smooth for a while — you feel just fine
You relax a little bit
Enjoy this time
But pay attention — presence of mind
You may discover the truth
Who knows what you'll find

Your motor might stop — too much pain
You need more out of it
Try again
So stand up tall and engage your brain
You've got to finish this trip
Tears are but rain

So settle down and rest my friend
On a good night's sleep
You can depend
For just ahead, around the bend
Your troubles will come
To an end

Twilight Zone

I'm nearing the end of my stay in hospital. That doesn't mean that I am cured. It simply means that I am finally taking on board all the information related to my condition. That information is designed to help me in terms of dealing with nightmares when they come, the shakes and the feelings of despair.

As I have said before, hospital and medication are only the first step towards recovery. The rest is up to me. I have been told that this could take years and will not be easy.

I have also been told that the door to Ward 17 will always be open to me should I feel lost again.

Limbo

Ever floated on a cloud?
Or even wondered if you'll get through somehow
Clouds are guided by the wind
Which way to go and where to begin

Backwards or forwards where do you go?
It's hard to decide when you're in limbo
You feel like you're ready or maybe you're not
You're feeling unsteady — best just to stop

Sometimes you're stronger — the best for some time
Then something takes over and messes your mind
Sometimes you're smarter — feeling awake
Then you look down and your hands start to shake

Why does this happen? Why no control?
What takes over your mind and your soul?
These questions make your blood start to boil
And this only adds to the rest of the turmoil

People have tried to help you — tried to explain
And the fact that they've helped only adds to the pain
For as much as they've tried to make you understand
It's not getting through when you're in that void again

You don't know where you're going — don't know where you've been
You're not sure of the future — don't know what you've seen
You're trying to go forward — to have another go
But it's so bloody hard — when you're stuck in limbo

Dad

'The Penny' raised a very important issue for me.

My father.

When I wrote that depression forces you to take a good, hard look at yourself, I meant it. You might find yourself delving into past memories that you thought were best forgotten.

Part of the recovery process is facing up to those memories and dealing with them.

So what you are about to read tells the truth about my childhood and pulls no punches.

Towards the end, I started to see things differently in relation to my dad.

By writing and publishing this piece, I am not trying to bore you with my life. All I'm trying to do is to let you know that sometimes by expressing yourself and getting things off your chest you begin to see things in a different light.

Victims

Born on the 18th of November 1952
I had just one older sister and a pet cockatoo
We lived there for quite some time — childhood was no bother
And somewhere along the line we picked up a sister and brother

By the time I was nine years old we had moved interstate
Although we were quite happy there — our opinions didn't rate
We staggered through this unknown land — not glad that we had come
It was here that I first remember the assaults upon my mum

Our father was a tall, dark man whose habits were quite rank
We smelt the beer upon his breath, when he lectured us it stank
Our mother was a working girl who slaved just like a maid
And tried to protect us all from his beer-induced tirades

Although they both had skeletons, we loved them like we should
But we'd cringe when the violence came, like we knew it would
And in the tender moments which really were quite rare
We'd gather like a family in the hope he really cared

By the time I was twelve years old we had moved interstate
And all the friends we'd made 'back there' — it just seemed they didn't rate
We didn't mind this new found land and thought we all could cope
But once again, the fights began to end our dreams of hope

Home was near a sandy beach which grew the tallest pines
The views from the surrounding cliffs, simply quite divine
This should have been a happy place that never took its toll
But that was without reckoning with my father's alcohol

When he was sober, my father could turn the charm
But provided with some alcohol he'd cause some bloody harm
At twelve years of age I challenged him, it was a move quite bold
And with a sledgehammer of a fist, he knocked me out — stone cold

The years spent in that seaside town should have been the best
But it was just another place — yes, like all the rest
Where we grew too scared to make new friends or visit other homes
For to do this meant more heartache — more pain before we'd roam

By the time I was fourteen we had moved interstate
And I'm glad I made no new friends — the one's that didn't rate
This time to a new land much further to the west
But it didn't really matter — it was just like all the rest

I found it hard to make new friends — the one's that didn't rate
It was hard to let them get too close — to let them call you mate
And girls were kept at a distance — their mothers would not approve
Of a boy from a violent home who would eventually move

While we were in this western town, everybody knew
Of the man of the household and his love of booze
His violent moods towards his wife led me once more to make a stand
And once again he knocked me out and thought he was a man

By the time I was fifteen we had moved interstate
And I'm glad I didn't leave behind any so — called mates
We moved to a country town that didn't offer too much cover
And somewhere along the line we picked up another brother

I told my sister I'd belt our dad if he caused the baby pain
He overheard me — dragged me out — knocked me down again
My sister tried to help me out and shouted some abuse
But he was the warden of our pen — it really was no use

As time went on we all left home — went our separate ways
And I have no happy memories of my childhood days
Except the thought that stepping up to challenge 'dear old dad'
Had saved mum and the other kids from the army belt he had

Why he treated us the way he did I could never understand
No one should grow up the way we did in the Promised Land
So I join the services, not for a job but as a means of an escape
I did my time, even went to war and started to meet some mates

Then I got married and planned not to be my dad
I wanted to give my wife and son the life I wished I had
But something went wrong — the wheels fell off — things were different now
And through a lack of understanding — I lost them both somehow

There are many more things that I could write about the following thirty years
About another failed marriage, the pain and all the tears
The sleepless nights, destructive trails, of booze and lost nightmares
Of suicide and loneliness and thoughts of sheer despair

For over that time I was violent — dependent on the booze
I was insular and selective of the friends that I would choose
I lived with different women but I'd always let them down
They'd wonder at the things I'd do — I'd leave them with a frown

So when I crashed and burned — when I fell apart
I was really forced to look at myself — right back to the start
Some thoughts are coming back again — to make the jigsaw fit
But it's going to take quite some time to bring back every bit

A large part of that jigsaw was my father's life
Why would he beat up on his kids and his darling wife?
Why did he drink as much as he did? Why did he need to hide?
Why was it hard to give his love? Was he along just for the ride?

An acorn doesn't fall too far from its tree
And since I've 'crashed', I've started to see a lot of my father in me
I'd followed that military path where you think that nothing's wrong
With the way you live and the things you do until it all has gone

The thing that sticks out like a sore thumb
— the thing that brings it home
Is after you've crashed — the help you get
— when my father could get none
For way back then, when the demons came they wouldn't let him be
And help was non — existent then — there was no PTSD

He didn't know or understand what opened all those doors
He didn't know why the nightmares came to remind him of the wars
He had no idea why he sat there — crying every night
And even though he beat his kids — he knew it wasn't right

He wrestled with the bottle trying to forget
He'd hide from his friends and family — hiding with regret
For to let them know meant weakness, a weakness you can keep
This meant more nights spent sleepless, more nights counting sheep

He died without knowing what the army did to him
He died without knowing that to seek help wasn't a sin
He died without knowing that there was love to be found
And when they lowered the coffin — no one uttered a sound

He left a wife who was battered in a tiny flat
And a son who's an alcoholic — suffered a heart attack
Two daughters twice divorced — never going forward
And a son who is finding his way in a psycho ward

It's hard to say I loved him for that would be a lie
And I'll never, ever forgive him — no matter how much time goes by
But now that I've travelled almost the same road as he had
I'm starting to see things differently in relation to my dad

He never had a chance — it was all preordained
It started on that day when he stepped out to be trained
Or maybe it was earlier when he was only a child
For what I'm led to believe — his father was quite wild

No matter how you look at it — he was trained on how to kill
Then they packed him up and sent him home without any other skill
He couldn't really handle it — fighting every bit
So he snapped and lashed out at things when nothing seemed to fit

So I guess what I'm trying to say — what I'm trying to get through
Is since I've crashed and sought some help I've had some things to do
Like coming to terms with my past and the problems that are at hand
So at this stage the best I can do is say, 'Dad, I understand'

I'm trying to unravel the mysteries of my mind
I guess they're the same as those that haunted you over time
I hope those that I have hurt will one day understand
Or at least take the time to look at what's behind the man

Just A Thought

I guess everyone's got a story to tell and you've just read mine up to the time I left hospital and got on with my life in the pages to follow, but before we go there can I at least ask you try to understand that everyone does have a story; some sad, some not so sad. Each story is a part of someone's life and is also part of the make-up that goes into who we are. Every one of us is an individual, yet we are all made up of our pasts.

In 'Victims' I have not singled out a particular person to blame, we were all victims, my brothers, sisters, mother and even my father.

My ex-wife and my son are now victims as are my grandchildren.

By writing 'Victims' I guess I am trying to say that, if my family or should I say ex-family, ever reads this book, they may get a better understanding of why they are victims and maybe fine — tune their efforts towards their own children so that they don't become victims too.

Party Time

I was lucky that I had friends who invited me into their lives and offered me a sanctuary for my recovery.

I speak of Cassie and Frank Luppino who live on the River Murray in South Australia and have a reputation for holding the best parties anywhere. Anything could, and usually does, happen.

After getting out of hospital I arrived at their place only to stumble into Cassie's birthday party. It was great to see a lot of my friends there and boy, did some of them play up.

Before we get to the incriminating bit, I should introduce the cast of characters:

Frank & Cassie (of course)

Darcy (great baritone)

Jackie (his wife)

'Pies' (crazy Vietnam Vet)

Di (his wife)

Tony (great drummer)

Heather (his partner)

Julie (party girl)

Bazz (another crazy Vietnam Vet)

Bob (me)

There were other friends at the party but the ones mentioned are the ones that stayed on till all hours and contributed something to the chaos.

Cassie and Frank's

There's a party on at Cassie and Frank's
You'll have a good time — put that in the bank
There'll be Darcy and Jackie with Pies and Di
And Bryce'll show up as time goes by

There's Tony and Heather and Julie too
But keep an eye on Pies — who knows what he'll do
With Bazz and Bob the night starts young
They're all well behaved 'til they're brought undone

The drinking starts slowly — they're all at their best
But when it's over they'll never rest
So to kick things off there's Tony and Bob
Singing off key — not a good job

But they don't care if their singing is too rough
They're having fun — you can all get stuffed
Frank is smiling — he's happy you'd think
Or has he just poured another drink

The pace picks up and Cassie joins in
And Julie rocks up — who knows where she's been
Bryce joins in to sing a song
And they all carry on as though nothing's wrong

The booze flows freely 'tween Bazz and Pies
They're getting pissed and so is Di
And Darcy's singing — now there's a surprise
He gets better with each tequila sunrise

Bob joins Julie to sing a few tunes
While Bazz lays down to look at the moon
Pies jumps on him and Darcy won't stop
And Julie yells out, 'It's stacks on top.'

Cassie's still singing who knows what she's missed
And Frank's at the bar — I think he's pissed
The party's still raging — could go on 'til dawn
When Pies falls over and head-butts the lawn

He gets up and scratches the back of his head
And Di just tells him it's time for bed
He staggers away and leaves us all there
And after a while we don't really care

'Cos we're still drinking and having fun
The way we're going we'll greet the sun
Slowly but surely everyone leaves
But Bazz, Bob and Frank drink on 'til three

Then Cassie comes in and says, 'This party's over'
We're all scared of her and run for cover
Bazz to his van and Bob to his bed
While Frank's doing damage to his head

At breakfast time the following day
We talk about the previous day
We're all hung over and feeling sore
But that won't stop us from doing it once more

Just A Thought

That party at Cassie and Frank's is one I will never forget because even though I had only just got out of hospital, nobody cared. They were more interested in the fact that the old 'gang' was back together and that we were celebrating Cassie's birthday.

In the coming months all these people had a big hand in helping me to adjust to my new life. The party also reinstated in me a renewed respect for the value of friendship.

Equality

I have been out of hospital for a couple of weeks now and, because of the friends I made whilst I was in there, I want to try to make it a habit to visit them and offer my support.

When I do visit them, it is sad to see that they still have to fight the same old battle just to get their entitlements.

One digger even joked that dole bludgers don't get treated as badly as Vets.

The Dole

Cancel Christmas — kick the habit
Easter's gone — let's kill the rabbit
Let's all cancel Australia Day
And who cares about the Queen's Birthday

Public holidays — who needs the role?
After all we've got the dole
For when you're on it day after day
Who cares about public holidays

Politicians think they've got it right
Providing funds for those in strife
But bludgers say, 'You bloody ripper'
Every day's now like Yom Kippur

To get the dole just fill in the form
They'll never check — that's the norm
Write down bullshit and other stuff
Then get pissed — it's the Melbourne Cup

And when you're broke — when your money's gone
Don't despair — just hang on
There'll be more next week for another tot
It'll be in your account — whether you like it or not

So if you're a bludger don't forget your role
Sponge off others and stay on the dole
Cancel Christmas and Labour Day
'Cos every day's a holiday

Author! Author!

In 'Words in the Dark' I wrote about depression as if it was exclusive to Vietnam Veterans and service personnel in general. Its scope is far more reaching than that.

I have written before about David Bean and what a great friend he has been to me over the years. His friendship and support continues in many ways. David encouraged me to read a book by an Australian author that had a title that certainly would not have attracted me if it were my choice.

To keep him happy, I took the book and read it and I am so glad I did.

If you have suffered or know someone who is going through depression or its associated illnesses then I thoroughly recommend this book to you no matter what walk of life you're from.

Mathew Flinders' Cat

I had depression for many years
And suffered without knowing why
I've stopped trying to hold back all the tears
And learned that it's safe to cry

I've hidden behind many a wall
Hiding away from my past
But you can only stay hiding until you fall
Then the walls start crumbling fast

You just get lost — can't see the day
Messages lost in your mind
You only think of dangerous ways
The mess you've left behind

Then you seek help to understand
What's happening to you
Professional help will set a plan
Give you things to do

But the best I've found came from a friend
Who gave me a book — take that !
Reading it showed a life without end
'Mathew Flinders' Cat'

So thank you David
For encouraging me to look
Into some pages of my life
Through Bryce Courtenay's book

Harping

Since I have been out of hospital, I have been fortunate that I have been able to visit the patients at Daw Park on a weekly basis. I trust these visits are helpful to them. I know they are therapeutic for me.

When someone is suffering from PTSD or depression, this is known as a 'thousand yard stare'. This means that they sit there so lost in their troubles and search within themselves for answers that they may as well be staring at nothing.

I know I keep harping on about these people having to beg for what is rightfully theirs but I seriously wonder what is more important, the money or the man.

The Thousand Yard Stare

You see them as they are coming in
You recognise it — know where they've been
Shoulders hunched — head is bowed
Shuffling feet — no way proud

Furrowed brow — worried look
You know the signs — it's like reading a book
Little to say and looking lost
He's walked the line, now he's paying the cost

You know he's thinking of the past
But you just can't tell him how long it'll last
You know he really doesn't care
You see it in the thousand yard stare

You've been there too — know what's in store
You try to help — tell him the score
You'll stand beside him no matter what it takes
'Cos he's got the signs — right down to the shakes

He's walked on through that revolving door
You've got to ask — how many more?
'Cos sooner or later it's got to end
They're dying off rounding the bend

This will suit the government well
They don't care about those that avoided the shells
They'll save some money — they just don't care
About those with the thousand yard stare

Decisions

I have been on many boards and committees in my time and I have to say that I think they are a waste of space.

They are formed to bring together business plans, ideals, community interests and other items that always affect someone else's life.

To save making a unified decision of the intricacies involved in each ideal or plan, they form sub-committees that are supposed to investigate issues such as planning, environment, budgets, etc.

They then bring a report about their investigations to the main committee. That's when the confusion starts.

The Committee

They've called a meeting of all their peers
For someone, it seems, has had an idea
That's solid and sound and may just work
So they've called a meeting to check out the 'perks'

The idea fits in with an overall plan
That has time frames and budgets that go hand in hand
So members have to be carefully picked
To cover each point — make sure it fits

To start things off they'll need a 'Chair'
Someone who's clever — with dignified air
They'll need members as smart as can be
And that's it folks — a working committee

Now they hold that meeting with all their peers
To sit and discuss that latest idea
They all gather to talk at the forum
But some have gone sick — they don't have a quorum

The meeting's adjourned to another day
When all can attend — have their say
And when that meeting finally takes place
Everyone's present — they're back in the race

Now perimeters are set to establish borders
The arguments start — 'points of order'
On some points, they agree not to agree
So they now set up a sub-committee

Their job is to look into relevant points
But they need a 'Chair' — who to appoint?
And when that's settled and they've made their choice
They go back to the committee that gave them a voice

Now that the borders have all been set
They think of how tight this just might get
For they've forgotten the budget — just didn't see
That they also needed a finance committee

With two sub-committees all's going well
The main committee's still ringing the bell
With finance and planning under control
They've forgotten about environmental

Now with three sub-committees all is in hand
The main committee's still running the plan
Now they know all's nice and ready
But just to make sure — we'd better go steady

They set an agenda for the next 'meet'
But once again, they're not all on their feet
They set a date another one
Where they can actually make their first decision

When they next meet — when they're all finally there
They're lost in confusion — even the 'Chair'
It's taken so long to set up the game
They realise they've passed the set timeframe

So they gather their papers and walk out the door
Sure they won't do this anymore
Disappointed they missed out on all the 'perks'
The only 'perk' they had was not having to work

Now the idea that was born is buried and lost
By a committee that couldn't develop a plot
So the best committee that I can see
Consists of two with an apology

Just A Thought

I must be honest. Not all committees are a waste of space.

I was a member of a rural City Council committee some time ago that was to look at the merits of putting walkways through a local swamp land. Good for tourism, the environment etc.

One member of the committee was particularly adamant about that, because we all knew what the swamp involved. We didn't need to waste our time visiting the area. All we had to do was make a decision.

He eventually pushed everyone until we had all agreed that the nature walk should go ahead. I thought it was a great idea then as I do now.

After the meeting I caught up with him and asked him why he was in such an all fired-up hurry to push the swamp land project through as quickly as he did.

He said, 'I had to Bob, because we've already put the bloody thing in place and I didn't need a committee to do that. They just had to rubber stamp it.'

No wonder he didn't want the committee to visit the site.

Angel

Do they exist?

Who knows? One thing is for sure and that is that at certain times in our lives, we all get into situations that could seriously harm us.

If we survive and walk away unharmed, we either consider ourselves very lucky or thank our guardian angel.

I'd like to think that we all have one.

The Guardian

I'm walking with you — you just don't know it
I've been beside you — watched you blow it
I've been behind you and watched you win
And tried to protect you from evil things

I've always been there — I came by choice
With you everywhere — even in your voice
I deliberately chose you at an early age
And tried to guide you through every stage

I've watched you stumble and I've watched you fall
I've seen when you're humble or standing tall
I've seen you at rest and I've seen you play
And at your best or even when you stray

I've seen you cry and I've felt your pain
I've watched you try and fall down again
I've felt the love that you have to give
And I've done my best to make sure you live

Yes, I've always been there to see you through
I've always cared about the things you do
For when alive I held you close at heart
And throughout time that bond will last

I've tried to hold you — touch you once again
But I understand that's not part of the plan
For my job is to guide you and not to show it
So I'll keep walking beside you — you just won't know it

Letting Go

Catching up with your friends and having the ability to visit those still in hospital certainly gives you the confidence to start moving on with your life. Whilst this is a very important part of the recovery process, you simply cannot move ahead unless you start to rid yourself of some of the baggage you have been carrying around with you.

Just let go.

Moving On

To move on doesn't mean to just stop caring
To move on is not to cut yourself off
It means that you won't stop sharing
And you can't control what I can't stop

To move on is not to be protective
To move on is not to deny
It's to let others be objective
To find a truth on which they can rely

To move on is not to change things
To move on is not about self
It's to fully embrace the things that change brings
It's to understand about your health

To move on is not to be judgemental
To move on shows no regrets
It means friends are not consequential
They're here for you — don't you ever forget

To move on is to fear less and love more
To move on is to know you've won
It's to face fear and to open love's door
It's to let go and to just move on

Cruising Again

You've already met Bazz, Frank and Pies. These three blokes have certainly done their best to live on the edge in terms of adventurism. Their latest effort is to cruise the Murray in South Australia from Murrawong to Goolwa.

This means crossing Lake Alexandrina which is a fair expanse of water that, at times, can be very dangerous. This danger is coupled by the fact that these three do not have a very good track record for successfully completing most adventures they undertake.

Usually something breaks down.

Frank, Bazz & Pies

It's almost noon, we'll be leaving soon
Time to cruise the Murray
We're heading south, towards the mouth
And we're in no real hurry

They've stowed our gear and packed the beer
Have Frank, Bazz and Pies
The weather's nice, they've packed the ice
And Bob's along for the ride

Into the day, we're underway
Cruising without any rules
Not too far out, there is a doubt
We need to get some fuel

With fuel on board, we head south once more
Let me give you the rub
With plenty of cheer we start on the beer
And stop at a couple of pubs

Now everything's right, we camp overnight
At the pub at Wellington
Pies and Bazz spend all they have
Again, the Pokies have won

Up at dawn, we leave in the morn
Everyone's feeling great
Cloudy skies, we're enjoying the ride
And finally cross the lake

Well the lake's been crossed, we didn't get lost
The Milang hotel we found
All's going well I'd like to tell
Except we ran aground

We're in the boat, back afloat
Now we're Goolwa bound
Nothings wrong, we fly along
Until the motor breaks down

It's not a race, it's snail's pace
Crawling across the lake
The motor's hurt, it just won't work
Now isn't that just great

It's got no power, so after many hours
Goolwa is in sight
After such a trip, we'll let it rip
Drinking beer tonight

Well we're all awake but its miles too late
The boat she don't want to go
What to do — we need rescue
It's arranged but it could be slow

It's all in hand, a rescue's planned
But there's time to kill alright?
We're stuck here so it looks like beer
Yep, we're back on the grog tonight

The following day we're underway
With a foggy head
The trailer's here, we load the gear
And wish we were in bed

We're on the road with a heavy load
The boat must weigh a ton
We're near the top when a wheel fell off
And brought the lot undone

Here's the deal, use the spare wheel
That's our saving grace
But as it transpired, we can't move the tyre
'Cos Bazz ain't got a brace

As you do, we searched for some clues
Looking for things that were lost
But all we found whilst hunting around
Was a pair of Pies' old jocks

To save the day, we called RAA
Who came and righted the ship
We set off again when it started to rain
And hoped the trailer would stay fixed

After travelling around, we found three more towns
We'd head straight for home you'd think
But with Frank, Bazz and Pies and Bob for the ride
We stopped in each one for a drink

After five long days, we'd finally made our way
To the safety of home for a rest
We've come back from the deep, all we need is some sleep
'Cos we're not really at our best

Now that I've been and I've seen what I've seen
I can honestly tell you true
If Frank, Bazz and Pies invite you out for a ride
Pre — arrange your own rescue

Busy

I have been out of hospital for one and a half months now and, in that time, I have played golf at Mannum and Murray Bridge (2 days), 'pottered' around with Frank and Bazz (5 days), attended the Clipsal 500 in Adelaide (4 days), driven to Horsham in Victoria (5 days), cruised across Lake Alexandrina (5 days). Caught food poisoning (7 days), followed that up with a dose of the flu (7 days) and attended appointments at the hospital on almost a weekly basis (5 days).

In between times, I've tried to add to this book.

Unbeknown to me, my friends had arranged an activities roster that was designed to keep me occupied whilst recuperating. I love them all very dearly for their efforts but enough is enough.

Sometimes when you feel ill, all you want to do is rest.

Rest

When I left hospital
I closed that particular curtain
And stepped into a future
That was at best uncertain

I looked forward to exploring
To search inside for answers
To understand where I was
To sort out all my cancers

The first few days went just like this
Close at any rate
Until my friends came along
I wasn't allowed to meditate

They'd arranged for me some things to do
Everything was planned
From helping them around the house
To Clipsal's racing stand

From playing golf or driving far
Or cruising 'cross a lake
To drinking beer in many bars
Everything was great

But after a while, it drags you down
You're not feeling like you should
It's all too much, all too soon
It's not doing you any good

So you have to learn to just say no
You're not feeling at you're best
And tell your friends you love them all
But what you need right now is rest

Solid

No matter what we do with our lives, there is always someone who will stand by us. Someone who will accept all our faults without question.

This person is solid as a rock and always will be.

Unconditional

It's unconditional
It began when you were young
It's not positional
It belongs to everyone

It's unquestionable
It makes you happy as can be
It's irrefutable
It comes to you for free

It's so reliable
Protection is always there
It's undeniable
It's from someone who really cares

It's indivisible
And everlasting bond
It's indubitable
It always makes you strong

It's indestructible
It can never be destroyed
It's unaccountable
For every girl and boy

It's unbreakable
It's the best there's ever been
It's not unspeakable
To love your next of kin

It's immeasurable
The amount there is to give
It's unconditional
The love your mother gives

Camping

I am a fortunate man that one of my closest friends is the award-winning photographer Barry Hartley. Barry and I have spent many nights out in the middle of nowhere just enjoying the ambience of a peaceful night by the campfire and enjoying the sights and sounds that surround us.

One night, Barry and I stood up to look at a spectacular sunset. Barry took a photo of it that showed a large tree trunk along the left-hand frame of the picture with two branches jutting out just above the setting sun.

Fingers Of Night

Flowers that bloom and open their eyes
To the warmth and glow of the morning sunrise
Birds that soar so high in the sky
Are welcoming sights to a weathered eye

Animals that walk neck — deep in the snow
Fish that go to depths that we'll never know
Oceans that will continually grow
Like daylight seeking that same ebb and flow

Mountains and valleys with rivers to cross
Trees with gardens that don't need a plot
Far distant places that have the whole lot
Remind us all of what nature has got

Yes, all things are beautiful in their own way
They all seem to offer the peace that we crave
But the image that, with me, will always stay
Is watching the fingers of night close the eyelid of day.

Characters

I met up with a couple of characters recently who both said that they had been everywhere and done everything together. Just name it – they've done it.

They looked a little soft to me, so I asked them if they'd ever lived in the bush or done any mustering.

They then proceeded to tell me the following story.

The Stampede

My mate and I got bored one day
City life untrustin'
So we hitched a ride and headed north
To try our hand at musterin'

Over tar and along dirt roads
Across this great wide nation
When the driver finally dropped us off
Ten miles from Red Back Station

After a while we settled down
No longer felt like strangers
They always make you feel at home
Up in the Flinders Ranges

One day the Boss came in and said,
"Boys I need some help
The water's gone — must move the stock
Up to Fishers well."

"Now the land is dry and pretty rough
So this warning you must heed,
Move the horses quiet and slow
Or risk a wild stampede"

From Red Back Station to Fishers Well
Is fifty miles or so
So we packed our horses with plenty of beans
Before we had to go

On the first night out the warning signs
Already started to build
A storm was brewing with wind and rain
And no shelter in these hills

So we stopped the herd and rode around
Ensuring all was right
With fearful wind and cutting rain
We stayed up most of the night

The herd had settled down by morn
But my mate couldn't take a trick
With stomach hurt and doubling up
He told me he was sick

Now to drive a herd one hundred strong
Takes two men or more
So he mounted up in frightful pain
And came right to the fore

We drove the herd through stinging dust
The sun had done its job
Its searing heat with fearful wind
The land — its water robbed

The second night out we stopped the herd
The sand and wind was howling
So we stayed up all night to quiet the mob
But my mate was seriously frowning

"It's getting worse — this horrible pain
Coming from inside
I'm having trouble sitting up
It's getting hard to ride"

His white, pale face and shaking hands
Left me with some doubt
If his condition should get worse
He may not see this muster out

But he reassured me — doubling up
He'd do what was needed
For we've been through dust, the wind and storms
And the herd has not stampeded

So off we rode with the herd
Everything going well
But my mate was getting worse it seemed
For his gut began to swell

On the third night out we rested the herd
On peaceful, grass — filled plains
We might get a good night's sleep it seemed
'Til my mate again complained

"My gut is near at breaking point
After all these miles we've rode
If it keeps going the way it is
I fear I might explode"

Then he doubled up once more
And release a noise so frightful
He leaned himself against a tree, and said,
"That was delightful"

He seemed to be a lot better now
His stomach had receded
But when he first let go that wind
That's when the mob stampeded

They ran through valleys and over hills
Across the great divide
They looked for bushes and caves and such
Or anywhere else to hide

They'd never heard a noise so loud
That rolled along like thunder
And never recovered from that smell
That took their legs from under

The herd was never found that day
Nor forever more
But I'll bet they never forget the time
They heard his stomach roar

Just Sitting

There's nothing like just sitting by a campfire with your mate enjoying a yarn and a couple of coldies and then finishing the night off with a nice red.

Embers

There's a feeling you get
Creeps into your head
Just you and your mate
Sipping red

The fire is warm
The night is calm
Just you and your mate
Causing no harm

You could be by a river
Or on a beach
Or out on your own
Just out of reach

Watching the clouds
Drifting on higher
And staying warm
From the coals in the fire

Think of those coals
Within that fire
That started as wood
Before the pyre

They're keeping you warm
And content within
You both stare in the fire
And think — where you've been

Yep, there's nothing quite like it
Just sitting around
And enjoying those embers
Right there on the ground

Stumbling Along

This book has happened by accident. A series of observations throughout my life, whether they be good or bad, have led you to what you read and are about to continue to read. It was never my intention to write a book. It just turned out that way. Another accident.

Most of the observations have come about through mistakes that I have made along the way.

The one thing I've learned about mistakes is that once you have made one, you can't change it. Just be sure to learn from it and get on with your life.

Mistakes

Mistakes always happen — they're not so rare
They happen to everybody, everywhere
Even to those with a duty of care
They're experienced by everyone, everywhere

Mistakes can happen almost every day
It might be in something you do or say
It might be in a bill you forgot to pay
Or perhaps forgot something along the way

Mistakes can hurt you, cut to the core
They can make you laugh, they can make you poor
They can make you cry, make the tears fall
But they're lessons really and nothing more

Mistakes aren't something you can hide in an urn
They're always there, not hard to discern
But don't let them cut you, don't let them burn
Just accept them all but make sure you learn

Mistakes are universal — they belong to everyone
And throughout your life, you'll make more than just one
So don't let them cloud you — bring you undone
Just learn from them all — then you'll know that you've won

Cobwebs

Over the past few months Bazz and I have spent a fair bit of time driving through isolated country areas of Australia and we keep stumbling on what used to be thriving rural centres, or at least reasonably-sized towns that, seem to have been forgotten.

Ghost Town

Retail store, grocery store
Guess we had the lot
Barber shop, mercantile
And shops where you could swap

Hotels that had restaurants
A place where all could meet
In a town that relied upon
The harvest of the wheat

Then cars and trucks came along
That went further on less fuel
And killed the rail that built our town
Our slow demise was cruel

A victim of progressive times
We slowly drifted away
And all that we left behind
Was a town that's in decay

Cobwebs and silence
Where once all was sound
And a wind that whispers through
What's now an old ghost town

Perfect

Isn't it funny how we sometimes feel the need to be perfect in what we do and say?

We seem to think it's important to be the best at what we do without understanding that by just being ourselves we are contributing more than we realise to living a meaningful existence.

The Broken Bucket

He walked up the road for twenty odd years
Carrying buckets — blood, sweat and tears
One was pristine, the other one broken
Just carrying water — not a word spoken

Down to the river every day
Filling the buckets without much pay
One bucket full — the other half empty
One was broken and one held plenty

For years, I watched him walk up that hill
Lugging water, though some would spill
The same old buckets from the time he'd woken
One was pristine, the other one broken

I stopped him one day and asked him why
He kept the broken one as time went by
He'd carry those buckets just like you ought to
While one was full, the other lost water

He told me that while the good one had done its job
Staying full while up the road he trod
The broken one always on the same side
Every day he walked as the years went by

He said that if I look back along the road
One side was dry while the other explodes
With colours and life that only flowers can give
It's the broken bucket that allows them to live

The flowers I pick whilst I'm still able
Fresh water and colour on my master's table
This starts him happy every day
To look after the workers that he must pay

The flowers are watered I say with some pride
By that broken bucket on the same side
Yes, the water that spills allows them to grow
This flows down the line to those that I know

I know that one's broken and in need of repair
I know it's not perfect and I don't really care
For it performs a duty without knowing why
By adding to life — no need to try

There's a lesson to learn here — a lesson for all
It doesn't matter whether you rise or fall
Just be happy with who you currently are
And understand — you're not a star

For you don't need lights to make yourself shine
And just like that bucket — it may take some time
To see the benefit of what it's got
It wasn't perfect — didn't carry a lot

By just existing, it fulfilled a role
Helping others, making life whole
Think of the life that has been awoken
Simply because that bucket was broken

Just A Thought

When I look back on how I used to be, I have a bit of a chuckle at how much of a goose I was. Always neatly dressed, always perfectly groomed, always conscious of what people thought about me and always wanting to be the best at everything.

I can now see that the only one I was fooling was myself. I now understand that all those things aren't as important as I thought they were. The important things, as I see them now, are friends and family, inner health, an ability to relax and an overwhelming understanding that I don't have to put on airs and graces in order to impress my friends. They either accept me for who I am, or they don't. It's as simple as that.

The River Murray

I have lived on or near the River Murray in South Australia for twenty years. It's in my blood. I've seen floods and I've seen dry periods, but nothing compares to the drought that commenced in about 2001 and still continues today (2008).

This drought has taken a devastating toll on the river and, to be honest, I doubt it will ever fully recover. It is the lifeline of our country and we treat it as if it were our slave. It's been that way for over one hundred years and we still haven't learned a thing about what makes it sick.

Before white man came along, the river ebbed and flowed as nature had intended for millions of years yet in a very short period of time, we have managed to bring this once-mighty maiden to its knees. Who do we think we are?

Now we have politicians arguing over who should manage the Murray, yet the answer is as plain as the noses on their faces. Give it back to nature!

It wasn't broke. Why did we think we had to fix it?

The Hundred Year Drought

Ever stood on the Murray and breathed in the air?
Ever thrown a rod in without a care?
Have you fallen asleep during the day?
Rocked asleep gently by the river's waves

Try to cast your mind back to the early days
When the river was alive in every way
Back to the days before levees and locks
When nature ruled the whole bloody lot

Now wind the clock forward a hundred years
And we haven't learned — we have no fear
She'll be right — no need to worry
We don't understand — we're killing the Murray

We're selling off water to foreign blocks
And we won't be happy 'til we've drained the lot
We thought we could manage — had no doubt
Until we were hit by the hundred year drought

So stand on that deck and breathe in the air
And throw that rod in but start to care
About our river and all its sorrows
And pray to God it's still here tomorrow

Get Over It

I met up with friend of mine recently and I asked him how he was going and if he had got rid of some of the guilt he'd had been carrying around as a result of his depression.

He seemed to give this a lot of thought and finally said that he had indeed dumped some of the baggage that he was carrying around. Especially the guilt he felt over lost loved ones etc.

He told me that it may take years for him to get over depression and Post Traumatic Stress Disorder, if at all, but he now understands that, no matter what happens, he has to get on with his life. Even those that he thought he had hurt will get over it eventually and move on to bigger and better things. It only takes time.

Cyclonic

Topsy, turvy, spinning around
Isn't it ironic?
Spinning pieces of our lives
Sometimes seem cyclonic

Cyclones travel unimpeded
Causing mass destruction
Destroying everything that they can
With no real compunction

Think of the damage we have caused
Without ever knowing why
Cyclonic damage throughout our lives
Leaving others to cry

Children and loved ones left behind
Sometimes you feel haunted
But after a while, you're sure they're fine
You carry on undaunted

For they've got theirs and you've got yours
Each a life to live
Just leave behind those lonely shores
There's plenty of life to give

Yes, throughout life you'll make mistakes
Don't be so catatonic
People get hurt along the road
We're all sometimes cyclonic

Organised

I have known people over the years that plan their holidays, weeks, months or years in advance. Then, at the last minute, something happens that causes them to postpone or even cancel their holidays.

We have no control on what's just around the corner in terms of life's journey, so I think it's better to be spontaneous and just leave when the mood strikes you. Wouldn't that be great? If only.

Plans

Have you ever made a plan to see the other side?
Have you ever dared to take a trip — take the car and drive?
Have you ever thought to get away — get away when you can?
Have you tried to do all these things — sticking to a plan?

Have you ever made a promise to travel without style?
To rid yourself of luxuries — rough it for a while?
To be as one with nature — face it like a man
Have you tried to do all these things sticking to a plan?

Most things are attainable in this world of ours
Just get out of your comfort zone — take your time and scour
Relax and take it easy — let your world expand
If you want to see the other side, it doesn't take a plan

Travel if you think you must, see what nature holds
Just let it happen as it should, let it all unfold
Pack your gear and travel, get out while you can
Travelling is for everyone and its best without a plan

Plans are just ideas that haven't had time to grow
So while you think about them, just pack your bags and go
Travel to that far off place that seemed so far away
And whatever you've forgotten can wait another day

For whatever is left behind can build up — let 'em stack
It'll all be there waiting whenever you get back
So kick back and relax, enjoy it if you can
And understand that what you're doing didn't take a plan

Hit The Road

I love to travel. The sights you see and people you meet certainly add to the joy of being on the road.

To be on top of the mountains on the coast of Australia, to sit on the beach and watch the waves roll in from over the Pacific Ocean or to experience the heat and dust of the Outback, brings a solitude and a 'oneness' with our country that all should experience.

It's a stress-free existence that offers opportunities to hit the road and discover your inner self.

Personally, I live in an apartment in Horsham, Victoria, and I use this place as a 'stock up' place between trips.

No Fixed Abode

Worldly possessions
Don't mean a thing to me now
Ownership and position
Have lost their appeal somehow

In this time of recession
It's time for the rest of my life
I don't need to make an impression
I don't need the trouble and strife

I've been there and done that
And I'm not going back again
I've got a future to look at
A whole new life to gain

My first impulse is to travel
And to see what's hanging around
Just to see what unravels
And never be homeward bound

For to have a home means security
It's harder to get away
I'd rather take off when it suits me
Take off any old day

I just want to travel the country
At a leisurely pace
With no timeframes to bind me
I don't want to enter a race

I just want to find out who I am
And I've got a long way to go
To make sure I learn all that I can
I'll have to take it slow

So I'll make it a recovery
To travel the country's roads
Whilst on this trip of discovery
I'll have no fixed abode

Travelin' Around

During my travels I have seen some terrific parts of Australia. I have explored South Australia, Victoria along the Murray, NSW and Southern Queensland.

Every now and then I see something that makes me stop for a second look.

One of those times was a farmer who had just finished ploughing a monstrous hill on his property. The furrows that he left on the hillside looked just like a ladder.

Stairway To Heaven

I've built myself a stairway to heaven
'Tho at times I was at sixes and sevens
From trying to protect the family farm
From nature's twists that cause us some harm

Over the years — labouring as you must
Blood, sweat and tears — from dawn 'til dusk
Sowing seeds and raising sheep
To hold it together without much sleep

Sometimes it's hard and leaves some doubt
Especially when you're hit by a drought
There's fire and flooding and sometimes famine
That stopped me from building my stairway to heaven

Then the rains come to replace those fears
So you scrape the hill to leave some tiers
That'll hold the water for the seeds I've sowed
Then I'm in heaven watching them grow

So you work the land when times get tough
And don't give in when it gets too rough
The reward you get for keeping things even
Is to look at that hill — my stairway to heaven

Upside Down

During my travels along the River Murray in Victoria, I came across a pub in the middle of nowhere. The Falcon Hotel is a beauty. Old fashioned charm and country characters that make the stop worthwhile.

Next door to the pub is a paddock where everything is upside down. Metal sheep and crows with their legs in the air and a tractor lying on its back. Even the toilet was upside down.

The Down Under Dunny

If down is up and up is down
And you see the roof lying on the ground
And your nose is always backwards runny
You might find yourself in the down under dunny

Where once was sky — is now the floor
Signs upside down on the dunny door
The wooden seat always dry and rough
Won't go down — always up

So accept it all and try to sit
Deposit your business and try not to miss
But if down is up and up is down
You find yourself looking up to the ground

Does what comes out rise or fall?
Or does it swirl forever more?
If it rises, does it fall up the sky?
Or does gravity take over as time goes by?

So after drying with paper in hand
You're left with one question, where does it land?
It's all so hard and not half funny
Trying to figure it out in the down under dunny

Welcome

In every state in Australia you find abandoned farm houses. Some recently deserted, some just relics of a bygone era. If the walls could only talk.

In my travels, I discovered one particular farm that was long past its use-by-date. In fact, it looked like it had been abandoned for possibly a hundred years or more.

The thing that struck me about this place was the sturdy building and an open door, still hinged, that seemed to be inviting me in.

Doorway To The Past

How do I tell you? Where do I start?
What it was like in the days of the carts
Just hitch up the horse — head into town
Do your shopping then turn around

Or ploughing the fields with the sun at your back
Horse dragging plough — attached with a strap
Cutting the crops was never a blight
As long as you always sharpened your scythe

Wife and the kids would open the door
And step outside to finish their chores
Like feeding the chooks or collecting the eggs
And saying their prayers before going to bed

That was then and this is now
And things are a little bit different somehow
The horses have gone — started to roam
And the walls are crumbling around our home

So the best I can do is to let you know
That as time marches on — things are let go
But the door will stay open — that will last
To invite you in — to look at the past

Gympie Muster

The Gympie Muster in Queensland would have to be one of the best music festivals anywhere. Great location, great choices of music venues, terrific people and plenty of laughs.

The last time I attended the Muster it absolutely poured for four days solid. There was water everywhere which made me a bit nervous as I had a camp near a 'long drop'.

The Hole In The Ground

When I arrived I was shown around
And then pitched my tent near a hole in the ground
The hole was the 'shitta' — a welcoming sight
For bladders that burst late into the night

Singing and dancing and ringing the bell
Vodka and brandy and Bundy as well
First night at the muster — partyin' on
Kicking our heels up and carryin' on

Into the night I felt some despair
Rising from bed to greet the cold air
Stagger away — not feeling too sound
To find some relief in that hole in the ground

Into the day — a day you can't miss
All laughing and singing and drinking some piss
Around the camp fire — all safe and sound
Which leads us back to that hole in the ground

Now, it's really not pleasant — the sounds and the smell
But it lets you know — who's not travelling too well
It gets lots of use — through the strain and the pain
But what happens if the skies start to rain

If the rains continue and start up a flood
The thought of that image just curdles my blood
The thought of what happens makes me go weak
'Cos though at the muster — I could be in shit creek

It's Out There Somewhere

On my travels I have had the fortune, or misfortune depending on how you look at it, to do a lot of gold prospecting.

First you need a detector, then a pick, followed by good advice about where the stuff actually is. There is plenty of advice around about where to go because nearly everyone you meet has a story of how a friend has found plenty of gold 'out there somewhere'.

The one thing you cannot buy in preparation for gold detecting is luck.

You sometimes have great expectations of finding gold just lying on the ground.

It's not that easy.

Gold

It's hard working in the bush
At least that's what I've been told
So hard working in the bush
When you're digging for gold

There's gullies and bush — so hard and rough
All day digging through hills
There's ants and snakes — and other stuff
Designed to test your will

There's granite and slate and old mine shafts
Then there's mineral waste
Detectors that don't quite fit the part
And a land you begin to hate

But you keep on digging and panning away
In search of alluvial gold
Or perhaps a nugget might make your day
'Cos there's plenty — you've been told

But the truth is really simple
I'll tell you if you're bold
You'll find plenty of the other stuff
But very rarely the gold

History

I have written previously about the number of small towns around our nation that are dying – becoming ghost towns.

A sad fact of history is that we have concentrated all our energies on helping larger regional centres to grow and develop at the expense of the little country towns. It seems that, the stronger the regional centres grow with the centralisation of police stations, hospitals, doctors, dentists and all other services that we depend on, the weaker our country towns are getting.

Another sad part of history is the fact that this centralisation has lessened our reliance on the rail.

We seem to have forgotten how important those two railway lines were to us.

Two Lines

Two lines going nowhere
That used to bring us life
Two lines going nowhere
Fade into the night

They used to carry goods to
Little country towns
Until time over took them
And slowly shut them down

They were a faithful servant
That took us to and fro
And gave some towns a life line
Until they had to go

But while they're lying 'out there'
There is a little hope
That they might come back to life once more
And not become a ghost

Right now they're two lines going nowhere
That used to carry life
Just two lines going nowhere
That fade into the night

Reliability

Travelling through the back of Bourke in New South Wales I came across an old Commer and I remembered that my Pop had one for years and swore by its reliability.

It was a small work truck that was designed for great workloads.

The Commer

I was built for endurance — not for speed
In fact, I was built to work
And I'm glad that I fulfilled that need
For that farmer — back of Bourke

He'd use me almost every day
From dawn right through to dusk
And I was always proud to hear him say
"She's a beauty — that old truck"

My life wasn't always easy
Let me give you the rub
Over dusty trails and boggy tracks
To 'crashing' through the scrub

But I did my job and tried my best
'Til the farmer told his son
"The old girl's tired and needs some rest
Let's leave her basking in the sun."

Movin' `Round

As I have said before, there is nothing better than moving around our wonderful country at your own pace enjoying everything it has to offer.

The freedom of living this kind of life is a feeling no amount of money can buy.

The Drifter

I've been a whaler — I've been a sailor
I've been a drifter too
I've seen the oceans — waves in slow motion
That's all I want to do

I've sat at tables — I have been stable
I've lived that life you see
I've worked the hours and had the power
But that's not the life for me

'Cos I'd rather ramble — I'd rather gamble
Just drift along with ease
Exploring the nation without hesitation
Doing whatever I please

No chains to hold me — No rules to fold me
Just like to travel around
I'm in no hurry — no need to worry
I'm never homeward bound

'Cos my home's the dirt road — my home's the tar road
Moving from place to place
Seeing what's out there — travelling without care
And leaving without a trace

I can't imagine — or even sanction
The thought of settling down
Can't think of going without ever knowing
What's in the very next town

Yes, I am a rambler — I am a gambler
I am a drifter too
I'll always travel — no need for rabble
Doing what drifters do

Bazz & Bob

Speaking of drifting around – there is only one better thing – and that's being able to do it with your best friend.

My old mate, Barry Hartley, often calls me when he is about to start another 'trip' and I always tell him to pick me up on the way through. It doesn't matter where he's headed. It's just good fun sharing the road and having a lot of good laughs with him.

Our friends have almost given up on us because they never know when we're going to be home next.

On The Road Again

They've travelled most the country
Snow, sleet and rain
Just happy to be together
On the road again

Going nowhere in particular
Happy just roaming 'round
From sunsets that are spectacular
To camping on the ground

From the Gympie muster
To the Hay plains
There really is no rest for them
On the road again

Two mates who have no timeframes
And no strings attached
Just drive on to the next town
Then unpack the rack

From the Flinders Ranges
To no place quite the same
Where they meet up with some strangers
On the road again

They love to sit by the camp fire
Tell a joke or two
And think about, over many a drink
The next town they're going through

So if you want to find them
I guess you're in for some pain
For they are travelling out there somewhere
On the road again

Respect

During our travels we always attend the Anzac Day Ceremony in whatever town we happen to be in.

It is pleasing to see the number of young people who attend these ceremonies growing every year. The amount of respect they show for our diggers, and what they did, certainly warms the heart.

Let's hope we never forget.

Eternal Soldier

Eternal soldier — on marbled stand
Forever guarding — rifle in hand
A victim of the world's past woes
Never forgotten — local heroes

Young men who all answered the call
To go and fight on foreign shores
Some came home and others stayed
Forever lost in lonely graves

There's a monument like this in every town
A sentinel set in solid ground
To remind us all not to forget
What led them all to eternal rest

They gave us the right to call Australia home
They gave us the strength to make it our own
They make us all stand up — shout loud:
Because of them – Australia's proud

So once a year when the bugle sounds
Get up early and stand your ground
And honour these men who paved the way
Honour them all — on Anzac Day

Observe

All throughout this book I have encouraged you all to look at the smaller things in life and to enjoy it while you've got it.

In the scheme of things, we are not on this planet for a very long time, so I think it is important to treasure every day you have which, for me, is a long step from where I was.

So I hope you understand just how important your life is and that you manage to observe all those things that we sometimes take for granted along the way.

Watch

Watch as your life starts
Watch life through your heart
Watch nearly every part
Learning every day

Watch as the dawn breaks
Watch as the day shapes
Watch how the sun shakes
At the end of day

Watch as the warm sun
Envelopes everyone
Watch how your life's run
Growing every day

Watch as the weeks fly
Watch as they pass you by
Watch how the darkening sky
Wipes away the day

Then watch as the years go
When you can no longer grow
Watch as your life slows
That's the price we have to pay

So enjoy life while you can
It's short — that's part of the plan
Live it — each woman and man
Encompass every day

Crumbling

During one of my trips, I received a phone call from my sister telling me that my younger brother had suddenly died.

After a trip spent travelling, partying, singing and, in general, having a ball, this news sent me crumbling to the ground. It was totally unexpected.

This news nearly took me back to the brink. It's funny how you go through life's toughest periods and survive and actually get to a stage when you think you are on top of things and wham! It knocks you down again.

At least I have been able to think about life as I travel along its roads and that helps me to cope, so at this stage I have had time to reflect on my brother's life.

Rod

Some said he was a simpleton
Some said he was a fool
'Cos he'd rather be with animals
Than spend his time at school

As a child he was always happy
Always playing around
And when Mum got mad at him
His smile would bring her down

He was never, ever angry
Always quiet and calm
And you could tell by the way he liked animals
He'd end up on a farm

For that's where he was happiest
Rising every morn
Milking cows and shearing sheep
A life for which he was born

He lived his life on the land
And worked as hard as he could
The hardest worker I've ever seen
With a strength of solid wood

From life he never wanted much
Just to be left alone
To raise and care for animals
Before he'd start for home

But sometimes it catches up with you
The hard work over the years
And on the night the angels came
Our hearts were filled with tears

He died a sad and lonely man
His life's work just begun
He had so much more to do
But he slipped away so young

So on the day we buried him
Buried him as we must
We put him where he wanted to be
We laid him in the dust

Now he's back where he is happiest
Let's all give him a hand
And remember him for who he was
A man who loved the land

Just A Thought

It's funny how, just when you think things couldn't get any worse, they do. Rod's death had a shocking effect on our mother.

Mum had always been our tower of strength. As children she would protect us from Dad's beer-induced tirades and resultant violence and, when we all grew up and left home, she was always the one we would turn to in times of trouble.

No matter what we did she always supported us and loved us unconditionally. We could never imagine life without her.

Crashing

It's hard to see your younger brother being lowered into the ground.

It brings back memories of his childhood and all the things we got up to together. These thoughts alone bring tears and pain.

We couldn't imagine, but were about to find out, how it affected our mother. She soon came crashing down.

Roma

After my brother's funeral
When all was said and done
We looked but couldn't believe
The look on dear old Mum

Her face was pale and sallow
Her cheeks no longer red
And a few days after the funeral
She couldn't get out of bed

She lost the will to fight
After all of life's hard knocks
And when she lost one of her children
That was the final shock

So we admitted her to hospital
Where she suffered day to day
But despite all the help she got
She quietly passed away

We remember a young, strong woman
Who gave us all she could
Who loved and protected us all
Like we knew she would

She was someone who was always 'there'
On whom you could depend
And her love was unconditional
Right up to the end

So now there's only memories
Flowers at the plot
And a world that's so much dimmer
Because of the love that we've lost

Scared

Mum used to tell us to enjoy the things we did, and not to die with regrets.

This thought often comes back to me now, especially when I see TV advertisements that tell us what not to eat and do. These ads all try to convince us that nearly everything we eat and do could kill us.

Well, hello!

One of the thrills of life is not knowing how long it will last. I wonder what people did thousands or millions of years ago when they felt a little off-colour?

There was no telecommunication back then so how on earth did they possibly survive?

Health

Why do we look at life and suddenly fear
All the things we once held dear?
Like eating foods we'd love to bite
And other things we've always liked

Ice cream and chocolates and other sweets
Even a 'burger was like a treat
Some people smoke and some drink beer
Enjoying their lives without much fear

Now turn on the telly and hear the news
They're trying to scare us with different views
On how we should live and what we should buy
Just to stay healthy — to live our lives

We hear them tell — what's good for us
But who do you turn to — who do you trust?
Will they make our lives all beer and honey?
Or is it really — about the money?

For me the answer's always been there
I eat what I want without a care
For life, to me, is no real mystery
It's been going on throughout history

It's all about time — back to B.C.
And even flows through to A.D.
People lived lives with what they had
It didn't matter — what's good and what's bad

For I think they were taught to understand
Life's real short — live it while you can
So they fished and hunted and camped by night
Living a life that would see them right

For they understood — that long lost throng
That their time on Earth wasn't that long
Yes their time was short in the scheme of things
So they learned to enjoy most everything

Over five million years we've lived on Earth
And always enjoyed each Earthly worth
'Cos there wasn't a doctor who needed the bucks
And there wasn't a telly on who we'd trust

Now we live in fear — each great nation
With the advent of communication
I wish we'd just get rid of the lot
Go back to mystery — we'd be better off

At least we'd enjoy all we could
Living our lives — enjoying the good
'Cos life's for living — not hiding away
Life to greet each new day

Just A Thought

Losing loved ones hurts, but sooner or later you have to get on with your life which, in my case, is by travelling and writing.

The important thing is to remember the good parts of the loved ones you've lost and to cherish those memories for the rest of your days.

So the memories of my brother and mother will stay with me as I continue to travel around.

Great Place

Harrow is a great place, just south-west of Horsham in Victoria.

The country surrounding the town is superb. Rolling hills, deep green valleys with creek beds that invite you to just sit and relax.

Another great part about the area is the Harrow Pub – it's a beauty.

Harrow

Travelling the country
Is such great fun
From Oodnadatta
To Jamiesons Run

From the Flinders Ranges
To Wellington
Or sharing a beer at Drovers Run

The pubs and people
You meet in each town
Lets you know
They're solid and sound

But the best I've seen
Straight as an arrow
Is the pub that's in
The town called Harrow

Redgum bar
And people of oak
They make you welcome
Each and every bloke

So if you think
You've seen the best of fellows
You haven't been
To a town called Harrow

Finale

Depression is not exclusive to Vietnam Veterans. It affects up to two-thirds of our adult population whether they be farmers, bankers, lawyers, housewives, secretaries or mechanics. No one is immune.

The unfortunate part about depression is that most people do not know they have it until it is too late. The nightmares start, the shakes start, avoidance starts, the drinking starts, you start crying for no reason and self-doubt takes over your being. Anything could trigger depression, so if you have these warning signs or know someone who has them, please remember that therapy is not a dirty word.

Writing this book has been great therapy for me. It has helped me to face depression head-on and given me an avenue that assists me in understanding it.

I have gone from a person who had everything in terms of a successful business and all the trappings that it brings, to a person who has absolutely nothing. It's been quite a journey and it's not over yet.

I've finally met someone I feel I can spend the rest of my life with and I'm so glad she has come into my life. **THANKS HEATHER.**

If my book helps at least one person through depression and PTSD, I will be a happy man because just to know that I have been able to help someone get through this horrible illness is worth more than all the trappings I used to have.

Wouldn't Be Dead For Quids

In this book, I've walked you through my trials and tribulations
They're no different to those of many people across our great wide nation
I've told you about the happy times and about when I was reclusive
Just like many sufferers throughout the land — depression isn't exclusive

I've led you through the darker times, always surrounded by doubt I've
told you about the hopelessness where it seems there's no way out I've
told you about the deep despair, never daring to think
And I've told you of all the warning signs that lead you to the brink

But if you read it carefully, it tells of times to come
It's there for you all to see, it belongs to everyone
It's about friends and family doing whatever it takes
And learning that to end it all is a stupid, stupid mistake

Now there is no guarantee you'll soon get well,
that's going to take some years
But if you talk about it with your friends, they'll help wipe away your tears
Just tell everyone what went wrong, what drove you to despair
You'll be surprised to find they won't laugh at you, in fact, they really care

The best way to manage it — depression and all its woes
Is to seek professional help that'll tell you which way to go
They'll teach you about the warning signs and about just what to do and
then they'll pat you on the back and say, 'The rest is up to you'

Now with the help of family and friends you can finally pave the way
To learn to relax and enjoy yourself and get better every day
But every now and then, you'll need to be by yourself, alone for peace of mind
For only by repairing yourself can you fix what you left behind

But along the way, you'll understand what friendship's all about
And family love that was always there, never really a doubt
Just remember those friends and family when next you hit the skids
With life to live and people to love — you wouldn't be dead for quids.

RELAPSUS RESURGEM

(When I fall I shall rise)